Fade In.

We're in a family room in the year 2023.

A couple in their early fifties are watching one of their favorite films on Turner Classic Movies as their teenage daughter walks in, sits next to them for a moment, and speaks.

"You guys are so cute with your old movies."

"Thanks, sweetheart," Mom laughs.

"Can I ask you something?" the daughter responds.

Putting the film on pause, Dad says "Sure. What's up?"

"It must have been so cool for you guys to have lived during a time when they still actually made new movies every year. What was that like?"

Fade Out.

Or Not.

It's up to us.

Bringing Back the
OLD HOLLYWOOD

WILD TIMES AND LIFE LESSONS WITH
SINATRA, CRUISE, REEVE, MADONNA AND MORE

STEPHEN SIMON

PRODUCER OF *SOMEWHERE IN TIME* & *WHAT DREAMS MAY COME*

Cover art and interior book design by Greg Traver at Command G. www.commandgdesign.com

Published in Portland, Oregon.

Printed in the United States of America
By Green Solutions, LLC, Anaheim, CA 92807

Cataloging – in Publication Data is on file with the Library of Congress.

ISBN 978-0-982 8201-0-0

First Edition.

Table of Contents

Prologue

"Hey, kid, want to taste something your Mom would never let you drink?" the older man asked me. I was four years old so anything forbidden by Mom was an irresistible call to adventure.

"What is it?" I asked.

"It's a soft drink called ginger ale," he answered.

Looking around at the guests in my parents' living room in Bel Air, California that day in 1950, I was proud to say that I had already tasted ginger ale. I was four, you know.

"Not like this, you haven't. Here, drink it all down quickly before your Mom and Dad notice."

With that, he handed me a small, short glass, the kind that I had noticed on the shelf in my folks' bar before. In fact, my Dad had let me drink water out of those glasses before when he poured himself another kind of drink.

"C'mon," he urged me. "Not afraid, are you?"

I had no reason whatsoever to be afraid. He told me it would taste great and it sounded like fun to me.

So I took the glass and downed the liquid in one gulp.

For a quick second, all seemed fine.

And then it seemed like I had just swallowed liquid fire.

My mouth, throat, and chest burned as though I was being assaulted by a blowtorch. My eyes got so watery with hot tears that they seemed to burn backwards into my eye sockets. The pain was so scorching that I literally couldn't even breathe. I started gasping for air but my stomach had told my throat to close up tight.

I felt my face get so red that you would have thought I had the world's worst sunburn.

The room and every one in it swirled around me. I had suddenly jumped on a merry-go-round that was spinning so completely out of control that I felt as if I was going to be flung away from the earth into outer space.

I remember seeing the smile on the man's face disappear when he saw the effects of the whiskey he had just given me. Then he walked away quickly. Very quickly.

Fortunately, another of my parents' friends witnessed what had happened. He saw me in distress and grabbed the glass so he could smell it. At the same time, he yelled out for my parents.

"Sylvan! Harriet! Get over here! I think Stevie's about to be really sick."

Almost on cue, enough breath came back into my throat and lungs for me to begin to simultaneously gag, scream, and get violently sick to my stomach.

From that point on, my memory begins to fade.

If I had been more conscious, I would have heard the kind man who had helped me tell my mother and father that it "was that sonofabitch Harry" who had given me the shot glass full of whiskey. I would have also noticed that Harry was no place to be found, having literally sprinted out of the house when he saw how ill his little jest had made me.

When I got a bit older, I discovered that Harry was Harry Cohn, the iron-fisted and almost universally despised head of Columbia Pictures from the 1920s through the 1950s. Cohn would also later play a prominent role both in my father's death and in Frank Sinatra becoming my unofficial godfather.

The man who helped me that day was Red Skelton, my Dad's best friend and collaborator, and one of the great comic actors and personalities of his day.

In 1958, when Cohn died and a few thousand people showed up at the funeral, Red was quoted as saying "See, give the people what they want and they'll show up."

For the four year-old Stephen Simon, the experience with Cohn was an important milestone in another regard.

It was the first moment I realized that I should never believe anything that a studio executive said.

Dedicated to the One I Love

This book is dedicated to my beautiful wife and best friend, Lauren.

I never would have written this book without her love and belief both in me and in the book itself. She is my rock, my cheerleader, my sounding board, my editor, and my refuge from doubt.

For years, Lauren, my family, and my friends urged me to write this book but, for various reasons, I demurred.

Lauren is, however, a patient, loving, and very persistent woman. One night, she said, "Honey, I love these stories. So do your children and your friends and so will countless others. The world loves Old Hollywood and you lived it. Heck, you are Old Hollywood! If you don't write these stories down, I'm afraid they will get lost and fade away forever."

In that moment of clarity from Lauren, I knew she was right.

She always is.

I also realized that The Old Hollywood itself can't just fade away either and the whole concept of this book took form right before my eyes.

You know that feeling you get when you suddenly realize that all your foolish defenses have just vanished?

That's how I felt in that moment.

For that moment, and for everything that Lauren lovingly shows me through the mirror she holds up to my heart, I am grateful beyond words.

Simply put, Lauren is the love of my life.

To quote that immortal philosopher Ralph Kramden:

"Honey, you're the greatest."

Introduction
The Last Resort

"Have you ever felt that the world is a tuxedo
....and you're a pair of brown shoes?"
George Gobel, *The Tonight Show*, 1962

Whither The Palm Trees

Near the end of the original *Rocky*, Rocky Balboa is about to fight Apollo Creed for the world championship. The night before the fight, Rocky tells his girl friend Adrian that he isn't fooling himself about his chances of actually winning. He just wants to be standing at the end.

In screenwriting classes, that scene in *Rocky* is considered perhaps the best example ever of managing expectations. Screenwriter and star Sylvester Stallone knew that having Rocky actually win the fight would really stretch credulity. He didn't want the audience to start watching the climactic fight with the sense that Rocky had to win in order to feel that he had accomplished his mission.

So, with a nod of thanks to Sylvester Stallone, it's important for me to share with you how I approached writing this book so that we begin this journey together with the same expectations.

First, unlike *Rocky*, I expect that we will win and that The Old Hollywood will rise again.

Second, I'm writing this book because I was born into The Old Hollywood, grew up in it, worked in it, and just recently realized that my entire life's work has been a reflection of my yearning to help bring it back.

I was indeed blessed to grow up around, know, and work with dozens of stars and personalities from The Old Hollywood.

I take no credit for that circumstance. I was simply born into it.

In that regard, I see myself as somewhat like the characters that Woody Allen and Tom Hanks played in *Zelig* and *Forrest Gump*. (On a personal level, much more Woody than Tom, that's for sure.) The lead characters in both of those films just seemed to find themselves immersed in fascinating situations with extraordinary people. I certainly had some wild times with them and I learned a lot as well.

Third, I hope and believe that my experiences will be both fun for you to vicariously experience and also give you a sense of who this guy is that is both making a passionate plea to bring back The Old Hollywood and also outlining some very real possibilities about how to do just that. (Chapters Fifteen through Seventeen).

I am indeed utterly convinced that The Old Hollywood itself must now re-emerge.

The spirit of The Old Hollywood was, at its core, a state of mind. As such, it can, (and in my opinion must) be renewed, relocated, and reborn.

As audience members, we felt the love of movies themselves from the stars, writers, directors, producers, studios, and crews that made The Old Hollywood films. There was a sense of passion, fun, drama, hope, and humanity that made us feel that we could go into a darkened theater and share the larger than life experiences that unfolded before us on screen.

Movies were our shared, national passion.

We miss The Old Hollywood even more when today we see the eighth sequel to some mindless action film, or the same formulaic story told over and over again, or comedy so crass that it embarrasses us, or violence so graphic that it numbs our senses, or the seemingly endless parade of dark, cynical, nihilistic films that masquerade as "deep" but in actuality make us feel ashamed even to be human.

Lastly, I discovered an exquisite metaphor that so symbolizes the massive transformation of filmed entertainment that we are now experiencing that it compelled me to stop fooling around, ignore the tuxedo of conventional wisdom, put on my brown shoes, and write this book.

More than any one image, the palm trees of Southern California have symbolized Hollywood to the world. Like the moguls who gave birth to the dream that was Hollywood, the palm trees of Hollywood were transplanted from far away places in the golden age of Hollywood during the 1920s and 1930s.

Those palm trees are now dying.

In 2006, the Los Angeles City Council decided that the dying palms are going to be replaced, not by new palm trees, but by sycamores and other trees more indigenous to Southern California.

When I first heard that, it made me very melancholy.

Now, however, I know that those of us who love and miss The Old Hollywood can take heart. The fading away of those palm trees does not in any way mean that the state of mind that was The Old Hollywood is also dying.

Far from it.

The dazzling images and memories of The Old Hollywood still resonate in our hearts and minds and beckon us now to be transplanted to new places and a new time.

Perhaps this is all most poetically explained at the end of the Eagles' visionary 1977 *Hotel California* album. The last song on the album, entitled "The Last Resort" contains the lyric:
"If you call someplace paradise,
You're kissing it goodbye."

The paradise of the Eagles' song was Southern California, the previous home of The Old Hollywood, not The Old Hollywood itself.

On one level, the adventures I describe in this book are both a reminder and also a celebration of the paradise that was The Old Hollywood, that marvelous place in which I grew up and worked.

On a deeper level, the spirit of The Old Hollywood is engrained in my soul and in the souls of hundreds of millions of people around the world. As such, this book is a passionate declaration that The Old Hollywood is most definitely not gone forever.

The Old Hollywood has faded into the mists, but like *Brigadoon*, it has been but cocooned, soon to emerge in a newer and more dazzling form.

I invite you then to join me on this journey to welcome back The Old Hollywood as it is reborn someplace else.

Actually, in many someplace elses.

That rebirth can come sooner than we can even imagine.

Because we are the ones who can now bring it back.

Stephen Simon
West Linn, Oregon

CHAPTER ONE

Nothing Succeeds Like Failure

"In life, honestly, I have failed as much as I have succeeded."
Jerry Maguire, 1996

Me, too.

For fifty-five years, I grew up and worked in the Dream Factory.

My Dad was one of the top comedy directors in The Old Hollywood, directing thirty-four films between 1937 and 1949.

I spent the Sundays of my youth with Dad's best friends Red Skelton, Milton Berle, Jack Benny, Abbott and Costello, and the Marx Brothers.

I played touch football with Elvis Presley, and my sister once dated him. Emphasis on the once.

As a teenager, I rode horses with Ronald Reagan on his ranch.

Frank Sinatra was my "godfather."

In my own thirty year Hollywood career, I fired Nancy Meyers, who went on to become the most successful woman film director in history and I also said no to Steven Spielberg.

A genius, I'm not.

I produced a film with Tom Cruise before he was *Tom Cruise*, made a classic love story with Christopher Reeve and Jane Seymour, and had more fun producing a film with Madonna than anyone with whom I have ever worked. Madonna gave me lessons in honesty. Yes, really. She did.

My producing mentors and bosses were Ray Stark and Dino De Laurentiis, the last two Old Hollywood mogul producers.

As a production president at the age of thirty-one, I had a blazing start to my film career. The first movie I ever championed, *Smokey and The Bandit*, cost less than three million dollars to produce and has grossed almost four hundred million dollars to date. (The real credit for *Smokey* as a film, however, belongs to its producer Mort Engelberg.)

I drove to my studio office every day, listening to the Eagle's song "New Kid in Town" and was absolutely convinced that they wrote the song about me.

I thought that humility was something you faked to impress women and advance your career. My ego stroked me all day, whispered in my ear at night, and then drove me into the abyss of self-destruction.

I married my boss's mistress and was blackballed in Hollywood as a result. In a heartbeat, the new kid in town became a leper.

I made hundreds of thousands of dollars producing movies, lost everything I owned in bankruptcy, and produced two movies that literally put the companies that financed them out of business.

I also had some very proud career moments and produced some movies that people actually saw.

Somewhere in Time, starring Christopher Reeve and Jane Seymour, has become a Cult Film Classic that has its own fan club. *What Dreams May Come*, starring Robin Williams, won an Academy Award in 1999. I saved a script from the scrap heap that became *Bill and Ted's Excellent Adventure*, a classic for teenagers. (Party on, dudes.) *Quantum Project*, starring John Cleese and Stephen Dorff, was, in 2000, the first original film to ever debut exclusively on the Internet.

Along the way, I broke a lot of rules and learned lessons that were at first painful and then ultimately exhilarating. I believe that the moments that haunt us most are the things we yearned to do but were afraid to attempt. When we try and fail, at least we know.

I've tried and failed a lot.

I've also enjoyed some other successes, such as the actors and actresses to whom I gave their first film role or a starring role before they became stars, including Tom Cruise, Charlie Sheen, Jane Seymour, Matthew Perry, Joaquin Phoenix, Julianne Moore, and Lea Thompson.

In 1990, my (then) wife had a breakdown from which she never recovered. We divorced, I declared bankruptcy, my home went into foreclosure, and my car was even repossessed out of my garage.

"Other than that, Mrs. Lincoln, how did you like the play?"

My family and career were in ruins, and my life looked and felt like a country and western song.

When I left Hollywood at the age of fifty-five in 2001 because I could no longer support my family there, I was broke, demoralized, desperate, and again deeply in debt. Another personal bankruptcy loomed.

I thought that my movie career was over. No, I *knew* it was over.

Wrong again. My career had only just changed forms and locales.

In the years since, I've had a lot of success because of those failures and my life is completely fulfilled and abundant in every way.

My failures in Hollywood led directly to founding a very successful movie distribution and subscription business that today has subscribers in almost a hundred countries.

I earned enough to pay off all my debts and also achieved my life dream to direct two films.

I met and married the woman for whom I have searched my whole life.

My daughters Cari, Heather, and Tabitha have grown into extraordinary young women and I am beyond honored to be their father.

My stepdaughter Brenna and stepson Carter have brought new joy, love, and pride to my life.

And I have a mischievous, adorable granddaughter Brianna.

All that happened only after I left California and moved to Oregon. Go figure.

Put another way, all that happened in Act Two of my life.

CHAPTER TWO

The New Hollywood: Act One
The Old Hollywood:
Acts Two and Three

"It's never too late to become what you might have been."
Away From Her, 2006

The New Hollywood is almost exclusively focused on Act One of the human condition. Much as the youth-obsessed culture of Southern California in which The New Hollywood is centered, The New Hollywood primarily makes and markets films to people under the age of thirty.

The Old Hollywood used to make films for all audience segments because it recognized that, like movies and plays, our lives also include second and third acts.

Every generation feels somewhat left behind and even abandoned when their time in the sun (the California metaphors just keep coming) is over.

Baby boomers (those born roughly between 1945 and 1965), however, have a relationship with movies and media that is unprecedented. We were the first generation to be raised with both movies and television and have no interest whatsoever in abandoning them or, perhaps more succinctly, in being abandoned *by* them.

Generations X (born roughly between 1966 to 1980) and Y (born roughly between 1981 to 2000) followed the baby boomers and have the same movie and television orientation as well; consequently, they will likely have the same desire to not be abandoned by movies when they move past Act One.

In fact, even the youngest members of Generation X are now moving into Act Two while much of Generation Y is still in Act one.

People who are in the second or third act of life (age thirty and over) still want entertainment that appeals to them and their interests, and these generations now have the power to guarantee that those desires are fulfilled.

The New Hollywood is not structured to do that.

The Old Hollywood is being called home to do just that.

By the time we hit thirty or so, most of us have lived through at least a few dark nights of the soul and, if we are honest with ourselves, we know that we probably will face those kinds of challenges again. We have, that is, looked into our own personal abyss and made adjustments that changed our lives forever.

But, as the curtain rises on Act Two or Three of our lives, we're still here, aren't we?

And so is The Old Hollywood.

CHAPTER THREE

The Old Hollywood, First Edition

"Life is like a box of chocolates.
You never know what you're going to get."
Forrest Gump, 1992

I was born in 1946 into an Old Hollywood film family.

It was the first year of the baby boom generation, and also the year after the United States had won the war that was supposed to end all wars. It didn't work out that way but that doesn't diminish the relief and satisfaction of that moment.

In the film industry, 1946 was the year in which *It's A Wonderful Life* was released. Now considered one of the best and most beloved films in the history of cinema, *Life* bombed both with critics and at the box office when it was first released. Almost every film I have ever made suffered the same initial fate. Some recovered. Others didn't.

My father, S. Sylvan Simon, had come to Hollywood from Pittsburgh in the early 1930s, having graduated from Columbia University in New York where he met and eloped with my mother, Harriet Berk. Mom was only nineteen at the time and had to sneak away from her parents in the dead of a New York night to travel cross-country with my Dad who had given up a law practice to venture into movies.

Talk about genetics. About forty years later, I also left the law for movies. A Jewish mother's worst nightmare.

Like the tens of thousands of servicemen who would, a few years later, fall in love with Southern California's weather and endless business opportunities, Mom and Dad were inexorably drawn to the paradise by the Pacific.

No snow. No ice. No smog. Blue skies, warm breezes, sandy beaches, bean fields, orange groves everywhere, and a movie business that was expanding with the speed of a new universe.

In the 1940s, California was indeed paradise.

The Eagles' "Last Resort" song was still decades away.

Those Were The Days

My parents arrived in Hollywood in the halcyon days of the 1930s, known quite correctly as The Golden Age of The Old Hollywood.

As did the country itself, Hollywood had survived The Great Depression of the late 1920s. In fact, Hollywood actually thrived during the darkest of those days as people had turned to film for escapism.

In 1927, Al Jolson had starred in *The Jazz Singer*, the first talking film. The 1930s witnessed the demise of the silent film altogether and the arrival of the golden age of films with sound. (Many of the silent film era's major stars were completely and often poignantly flummoxed when they had to actually start speaking on screen.)

In 1930, Jean Harlow starred in *Hell's Angels*, Howard Hughes' epic film. At a cost of three million dollars, it was by far the most expensive film ever made to that date.

Greta Garbo spoke on screen for the first time in *Anna Christie* (1930).

Clark Gable and Joan Crawford made *Dance, Fools, Dance* (1931), the first of their eight films together.

Katherine Hepburn made her screen debut in *A Bill of Divorcement* (1932).

John Wayne made his western movie debut in *The Big Trail* (1932), followed a few years later by his first huge western hit *Stagecoach* (1939).

Olympic swimming star Johnny Weissmuller made his film debut in *Tarzan, The Ape Man* (1932).

Shirley Temple starred in her first short film *Baby Burlesk* (1933).

The Three Stooges made *Woman Haters* (1934), the first of their almost two hundred comedy films over the next twenty-five years.

Popeye (1933) and *Donald Duck* (1934) appeared in their first cartoons.

Becky Sharp (1935) became the first full-fledged Technicolor film. The first all-Hollywood publication, the Hollywood Reporter, debuted in 1930.

In 1935, the New York Society of Film Critics was created, thus launching a whole new field of psychotherapy for filmmakers who receive bad reviews. (Thank God my wife is a therapist.)

The world's first drive-in theater (aka "passion pit") appeared in Camden, New Jersey in 1933.

A year later, Southern California got its own first drive-in on Pico Boulevard in West Los Angeles. I could say that I saw many a film there until its demise in the 1970s but really, did anyone under twenty-one ever actually *watch* a film at a drive-in?

The decade culminated in 1939 as a record six hundred and fifty films were produced, including the ageless classics *Gone With The Wind* and *The Wizard of Oz.*

That was The Old Hollywood at its zenith.

Where Dinosaurs Roamed: Reign Of The Studios

In the Old Hollywood film culture, the studio itself was everything.It's hard to imagine today but back then, studios engendered great loyalty from actors, directors, writers, producers, and movie crews themselves.

People proudly talked about being a part of the MGM family, or the Fox family, etc. Disputes, rivalries, and broken hearts existed, of course, but the studio system itself was the backbone of the industry.

And the studios took their responsibilities to the public very seriously. They developed genres like gangster films, musicals, westerns, romantic comedies, fantasies, and action films, which they turned out by the hundreds, appealing to every audience segment.

Most crucially, story telling was paramount.

Yes, *movie stars played roles in films but they were hired to service the story, rather than the other way around* as it is in so many of today's movies. Movie stars were exalted, yes, but the script was still the core around which the stars rotated.

To service, respect, and protect that core in The Old Hollywood, studios had extensive story departments and screenwriters were actually respected and much sought after. Writers were so revered that the competition to get writers under contract was almost as fierce as the competition for stars.

In The Old Hollywood, studios and powerful producers such as David O. Selznick (*A Tale of Two Cities, Anna Karenina, A Star is Born*) were the prime developers of scripts.

In The Old Hollywood, actors, producers, writers, and directors were under contract to studios and had fewer choices about which films they worked on. As a result, they often made three or even four films a year. (My father directed and produced forty-three films between 1937 and 1950, which averages out to about four films per year.)

All costs were borne by the studios and all profits were retained by the studios.

The studio chiefs in The Old Hollywood were focused only on movies, not television, cable, DVDs, or theme parks, none of which existed.

Most of those studio heads (like Louis B.Mayer, Irving Thalberg, Darryl Zanuck, and yes, even Harry Cohn) had a passion for movies. They loved movies, movie stars, and the entire process of getting films made. The Old Hollywwood was not just a business to them; rather, it was an expression of what they loved most to do in life.

In the Old Hollywood, some of the studios even owned their own chains of movie theaters. That ended in the late 1940s with the famous consent decree that forced the Warner brothers to choose between production and exhibition. At one point, the trial judge told Jack Warner that he and his brothers would have to choose between owning the studio and owning the theaters. Warner's supposed response: "We've figured that out, your honor. I'm keeping the studio and my brothers are keeping the theaters." Good try, Jack.

In The Old Hollywood, movie stars were larger than life in every way. Yes, there were still scandals and foibles but, for most of the public, those moments flamed brightly and quickly disappeared.

In the studio era, the prime focus of full-time publicists was as much to keep a star's name out of the news as it was to lionize them.

Fortunately, the twenty-four hour news cycle didn't exist, nor did television, cable, the Internet, or the now countless, breathless shows and websites dedicated to celebrity minutiae.

As a consequence, it was still possible in The Old Hollywood to create and maintain an aura of mystery or privacy about movie stars.

The Old Hollywood would not have enjoyed the mystique it possessed if TMZ.com had been around then.

The Old Hollywood was still fresh and flush with ideas during the

1930s and the 1940s. After all, talking films had only been around since 1927 and there were still thousands of new stories and new vistas to explore.

The Old Hollywood also had a virtual monopoly on visual entertainment; therefore, it reigned supreme.

Television was only in its very early experimental stages and was still a decade away from even debuting in American homes.

There were no video games, DVDs, computers, or texting. In other words, people actually talked to each other more. Imagine that.

Live theater existed on Broadway in New York, but the day of the traveling theatrical road show of a Broadway success was still many years in the future.

News and sports in the 1930s and 1940s were confined to radio and newsreels.

With no real visual entertainment competition, movies were indeed *the thing.*

Little did the studio chiefs know at the time, but that was the last decade in which they would hold that exclusive, non-competitive status.

We'll look at how differently the New Hollywood operates in Chapter Fifteen.

Sunrise on Sunset

It was into The Old Hollywood that my Dad immersed himself.

He got various jobs as a drama coach, radio executive, and stage director before he signed on at Warner Brothers in 1935 to direct screen tests. He then moved to MGM as a director and assistant director in 1937 where he began a twelve-year run of directing hit comedies.

Mom and Dad bought a home on the legendary Sunset Boulevard in Bel Air. The same Sunset Boulevard that would in 1950 be immortalized by the film of the same title and Gloria Swanson's classic "I'm ready for my close-up, Mr. deMille."

Our house was just a couple of blocks west of Beverly Glen Blvd., that led into the hills of Bel Air and which would, many years later, wind its way into the vast San Fernando Valley on the other side of the Santa Monica Mountains.

Sunset Boulevard stretched from downtown Los Angeles all the way to the beach, making it (at that time) one of the few east/west routes from the city to the beach.

Midway between downtown and West Los Angeles, Sunset made its way through Hollywood, just south of Hollywood Boulevard itself.

In the West Hollywood stretch of Sunset, you could stop at Schwab's famous drug store, the site of so many real and imaginary star discoveries.

Charlie Chaplin even made his own sodas there in the 1930s.

Lana Turner, with whom Dad made two films, later claimed that her discovery at Schwab's was an urban myth but the legend remains. As in most things "Hollywood", the image is far more important than the truth.

Moving west, the Sunset Strip would come into view.

The Strip burst first into national recognition in the famous 1958-1964 television series *77 Sunset Strip*, which introduced Edd "Kookie" Byrnes and his ubiquitous comb to a waiting world.

The Strip's Whisky A-Go-Go and Pandora' s Box would later in the 1960s become the Los Angeles epicenter of the music and lifestyle revolution.

Sunset then winds through Beverly Hills. If my parents looked closely enough, they could see the young palm trees planted along Sunset during the 1920s and 1930s, particularly around The Beverly Hills Hotel, which still stands there today.

Sunset then moves past my parents' old house and serves as the northern border of UCLA, in the exact location of Jan and Dean's 1964 hit song, "Dead Man's Curve."

Sunset then snakes along through Brentwood and Pacific Palisades and ends on the sands of the Pacific Ocean.

My Sister, My Hero

In 1938, Mom and Dad welcomed their first child, my sister Susan, into that house on Sunset. (The house, now behind a brick wall and rebuilt, is still there.)

Susie was witness to the real heyday of Dad's career, the 1940s.

She appeared in brief cameos in many of Dad's films and, as long as she kept up with her homework, she got to hang out with him at MGM.

In a way, the MGM lot was the 1940s version of today's Universal Studios Tour, except that it wasn't open to the public.

MGM's back lot stretched over almost two hundred acres and

featured complete western sets, whole towns, prison sets, the *Showboat* area that included a huge lake, Andy Hardy Street, twenty-eight sound stages, and countless warehouses.

Susie's particularly favorite treat was being able to swim in the tank that had been built for Esther Williams.

Susie, whom I called Tudie when I was young and couldn't pronounce an "s", was and still is my hero. She was eight years old when I was born and she has loved, defended, and supported me all my life. We have never had so much as one argument and I simply adore her.

It is, then, I'm sure, one of God's happy little jests that Susie has gone on to become the very successful film critic Susan Granger.

A filmmaker with a sister who is a film critic is somewhat akin to a tree lover whose sister is a lumberjack.

My Dad: Forty-Three Films in Thirteen Years

Between 1937 and 1949, Dad directed thirty-four films, and became one of the go-to comedy directors of The Old Hollywood.

He directed several films with his best friend Red Skelton, such as *Whistling in Brooklyn, Whistling in Dixie* (was that the beginning of sequels?) and *The Fuller Brush Man.*

Dad also directed:

Her Husband's Affair with Lucille Ball, and he later produced *The Fuller Brush Girl* in which Ball starred as well.

Song of The Open Road in which a young girl named Suzanne Burce made her film debut as a character named Jane Powell. Louis B. Mayer liked the name so much that he insisted she adopt it as her own for the rest of the career. Jane married former child star Dickie Moore and has become one of my sister's best friends. Recently, Lauren and I had the pleasure of having dinner with Jane, Dick, and my favorite brother-in-law James Mapes at my sister Susie's home in Connecticut. James is actually my only brother-in-law but even if I had another one, Jim would still be my favorite.

Bad Bascomb with Wallace Beery, which also introduced Margaret O'Brien in her first feature film.

Rio Rita with Abbott and Costello and *Dancing Coed* with Lana Turner.

Between 1948 and 1950, he also produced nine films, including *Abbott and Costello in Hollywood* and *Born Yesterday,* for which Judy Holliday won the Oscar for Best Actress.

On March 9, my Dad's birthday, Robert Osborne of Turner Classic Movies often devotes a whole day of programming to his movies.

Madhouse: Berle, Benny, Skelton, Abbott, Costello, and The Marxes

It was into that house on Sunset Boulevard that I was born on June 30, 1946.

In the late 1940s, our home became the clubhouse (although my mother later told me that "madhouse" would have been a more appropriate description) where my Dad, Red Skelton, Milton Berle, Jack Benny, George Burns, Gracie Allen, Bud Abbott, Lou Costello, Groucho Marx, Harpo Marx, and others gathered almost every Sunday afternoon to barbecue hot dogs and hamburgers and to hang out with my Dad, my mother, my sister Susie, and a very young me.

They also used to watch movies and dailies (rough footage shot each day on a movie set) in Dad's projection room which was right next to the pool and where a sign on the door read: Simon Bijou Theater.

Susie watched dailies a lot with Dad in that room and, even though I was quite young, I remember sitting on Dad's lap and watching images on the screen that I didn't really understand. I did know, however, that Daddy had created them.

Now, about those Sunday guests.

Uncle Red (Skelton) was Dad's dearest friend and constant collaborator. I was told to call them all Uncle something-or-other. There were a lot of uncles but no "aunt" until later when Lucille Ball became friends with my mother.

In 1951, Red launched his CBS television show that became a mainstay of network television for twenty years.

Not to be outdone, Uncle Miltie (Berle) was just adapting the television version of his radio *Texaco Star Theater* from radio to television. When his show launched in 1948, the whole medium of television was almost instantly transformed from a novelty into a national passion.

Milton's Tuesday night show was such a huge hit that he regularly attracted as much as eighty per cent of the available television audience and, in the first known instance of television's impact on movie attendance, theater owners actually complained that fewer movie tickets were sold on Tuesdays.

Sales of television sets themselves more than doubled the year after Uncle Miltie's show debuted. (We had no exclusivity calling him Uncle Miltie. He was known as that to everyone who watched his show.)

Uncle Bud (Abbott) and Uncle Lou (Costello) were already huge movie stars and were also about to launch their own television show, which became a huge success. Their "Who's on First?" comedy sketch is known as one of the classic routines in the history of comedy.

As to the Marx Brothers, Dad supervised some of the slapstick sequences in *The Big Store* and the Marxes consulted with him on big comedy set pieces in some of their other films.

Harry Cohn, Sinatra, and Dad's Death

Later, Dad was the Vice-President of Production at Columbia under Harry Cohn where he was responsible for the purchase and initial development of *From Here to Eternity*, a highly acclaimed and best-selling novel by James Jones (who also spent a lot of time in our house).

Trying to cast Frank Sinatra in the film, Dad ran afoul of Harry Cohn who was furious with Sinatra. Cohn had a quick change of heart and, even though he didn't explain what my father had done for him until my eighteenth birthday, Frank Sinatra became my unofficial godfather and benefactor for the next thirty years.

Dad died suddenly in 1951 at the age of forty-one.

The news stories both at the time and since called the cause of death a heart attack, but that was merely a family cover story. For many years, my mother insisted to me that Dad had worked himself into the heart attack that killed him. I actually believed that explanation until I was twenty-three years old when, through a serendipitous encounter with Red Skelton, I learned and then later confirmed the truth.

We'll look at what Red told me and also discuss the Sinatra and Skelton connections in depth in Chapter Four.

Dad worked almost around the clock at Columbia Pictures under the tyrannical Cohn. Worried that my father would actually work himself to death, my mother had actually begged Cohn to fire my father but he refused. As a result, my mother left my father to make a point to him of his growing addiction to work and also to the painkillers he was taking for migraine headaches.

Never intending to really leave permanently, she went to dinner with Ray and Fran Stark at their house, which was less than a mile away, and then checked in for one night at the nearby Bel Air Hotel. As fate would have it, Dad died suddenly the next morning. My fifth birthday was one month away.

My mother was understandably crushed with guilt. She also then discovered that Dad had kept an apartment in another part of town for assignations with a series of girlfriends. She also learned that, due to their extravagant lifestyle, she had very little money to keep her, my sister, and me going.

Mom really had a hard time dealing with all that and just couldn't bring herself to actually tell me that Dad had died, so she made up a wild story about Dad having gone on a long business trip.

After several months of complaining to my mother about that ruse, Susie, who was by then thirteen, was the one who actually sat me down in our backyard and explained that Dad had died.

On the same morning my Dad died, his protégé and dear friend Ray Stark went to Columbia to clean out Dad's desk so that no one would ever find any proof of the painkillers that Dad was taking.

Ray was still an agent at the time. His wife Fran was Fanny Brice's daughter. Ray later came up with the idea for *Funny Girl*, which he produced, and went on to become both one of the most successful and feared producers ever in Hollywood (*The Way We Were, Annie, The Goodbye Girl*, etc.) and also my mentor.

A New Name

Only seven months after my father's death, my mother married Armand Deutsch, one of the heirs to the Sears Roebuck fortune.

Whereas her relationship with my birth father had certainly been born of love, her remarriage so soon after Dad's death had a lot more to do with money and security. Her quick remarriage also alienated her from many of my birth father's closest friends, including Red Skelton.

Ardie (as his friends called him) was a very reserved and totally decent man who had gained an odd notoriety when he revealed that he, as a child, had been the initial kidnapping target of Loeb and Leopold, not Bobby Franks whom they tragically kidnapped and murdered.

My stepfather, who was introduced to my mother by Ray and Fran Stark only a few months after my Dad's death, also had become a film producer, making films like *Green Fire* with Grace Kelly and *Saddle The*

Wind with Robert Taylor, a very young John Cassavetes, who became one of my first mentors, and Julie London, who became the first major crush of my life. I was twelve at the time.

My stepfather adopted me and the Simon name disappeared until I reclaimed it fifty years later.

So that is a glimpse of The Old Hollywood into which I was born.

There will be much more on what it was like to grow up in that world, or at least try to, in Chapter Five.

As you will now discover, the actual process of growing up was not something I did very well at all.

CHAPTER FOUR

My "Godfather" Frank Sinatra

"I'm going to make him an offer he can't refuse."
The Godfather, 1972

The Sinatra Gifts

When my mother married my stepfather in December 1951, we moved from our home on Sunset Boulevard in Bel Air into a huge house on Bedford Drive in Beverly Hills, just north of Sunset and just west of the Beverly Hills Hotel. My stepfather had bought the home from its previous inhabitants, Ava Gardner and Artie Shaw.

Being north of Sunset was a big status symbol at that time. If you lived in the north, it meant that your family had real money.

As obnoxious as that was, neighborhood teams for touch football games would often be chosen based on norths and souths. Of course, that perspective failed to recognize that basically every one who lived in Beverly Hills was much better off financially than ninety-nine per cent of the country. This was West L.A., however, and, in that Hollywood state of mind, perception is and always has been more important than reality. That state of mind also completely distorted my youth. I thought every one grew up with maids, butlers, and first class travel anywhere in the world.

My stepson Carter still takes great delight in calling me Butler Boy.

Our section of Bedford Drive, with only ten houses, was quite an interesting Hollywood block on which to live.

Famed director Jean Negulesco (*Three Coins in a Fountain*, *How to Marry a Millionaire*) and his wife Dusty lived right next door to us and hosted weekly croquet games in their backyard.

Comic Ed Gardner, star of both the radio and television versions of *Duffy's Tavern* ("where the elite meet to eat") lived two houses north.

The extraordinary composer John Green, who was then the Music Director at MGM (*West Side Story, Bye-Bye Birdie*), lived with his wife Bonnie across the street, as did producer Joe Cohn, who was one of the founding members of The Academy of Motion Picture Arts and Sciences. Joe had a houseman with the wonderfully improbable name of Zany, who made cookies or brownies almost daily for the kids on the block.

And the street was, of course, lined with palm trees.

It was soon after moving onto that block that I began to be aware that I had a very special benefactor named Frank who always gave me amazing gifts on my birthday and Christmas.

For instance, on one birthday, an entire electric set train set arrived at our house. Not just trains, either. There were bridges, cities, mountains, and lakes that took up most of the floor space in my room. On other occasions, I received gifts like a new Schwinn bicycle and a complete stereo set.

Every birthday, every Christmas, without exception, I would get the kind of gift that any young boy fantasized about from "Uncle" Frank.

Frank's largesse led to some pretty heated discussions between Frank and my stepfather who felt that Frank was somehow one-upping him at every turn. That was their problem. I loved it.

As I got a bit older, I became aware that Frank's last name was Sinatra.

Frank was present for dinner parties at our home on Bedford and also in the home my parents later built on a private hill, right near the fire station that marked the boundary of Beverly Hills and the beginning of Coldwater Canyon, which ended in the San Fernando Valley.

No one, however, admitted actually going to the "Valley" at that time. As colossally silly and snobbish as it was, Westsiders saw the valley as a kind of no-persons-land, situated on a distant planet where the people, such as they were, spoke in a foreign language and used a different currency.

An ironic aspect of Frank being a frequent guest at our new house was that his ex-wife Nancy lived literally right next door. We referred to the ex-Mrs. Sinatra as Big Nancy so as to distinguish her from Little Nancy, Frank's daughter, whose boots were made for walking. There were three lots on the hill where my parents built their home and Big Nancy's house was one of the three.

I knew Little Nancy slightly, but I don't remember being around Frank, Jr. at all. They were both older than me. Frank's youngest daughter Tina was, however, only two years younger than me and we did spend a little time together during those years.

Truth be told, I had a major crush on Tina when we were both in our late teens but I knew the feelings weren't reciprocal and I was terrified by the thought of ever upsetting Sinatra. I therefore "crushed" in silence. In March 2009, an article written by Todd Purdum entitled "The Children of Paradise" was published in *Vanity Fair*. When Todd interviewed me for the article, I told him about my Tina crush and he then told her. "Oh, Steve said that? That's adorable," Tina is quoted as responding. As to my fear of upsetting her Dad? "I don't blame him. I would have been, too."

On my sixteenth birthday, I became aware of a huge argument between my stepfather and Frank about who was going to buy me my first car.

My stepfather won the argument with Frank and I started driving a new, 1962, black convertible Ford Galaxy. Yes, that was the consolation prize.

Sometimes I look back at those days and remember the Bob Seger line from his classic song, "Against the Wind":

"I wish I didn't know now what I didn't know then."

Spoiled? As Miss Piggy would say, "Moi?"

1962 was also a time when I was becoming increasingly enamored of the lifestyle and attitude of both Sinatra and also Ray Stark, the famed movie producer who would later play such a huge role in my own career. My stepfather was alarmed that, by emulating those two men, I was heading in what he thought of as a wild and unpredictable direction. Like to the film business, maybe? What a shock that would have been, right? My Dad had been a producer/director and my stepfather had been a producer. Of course that would naturally lead me into a career as a…stockbroker? As if.

Anyway, I had no idea why I received all these great gifts from Uncle Frank.

I was just grateful that they kept coming.

Sinatra Lifts The Veil

Right around my eighteenth birthday (June 30,1964), I was summoned to Frank's house, and finally discovered why Frank had been so incredibly kind to me.

When I arrived, Frank was standing out in front, leaning on a new, silver, convertible, 1964 Corvette Stingray, the ultimate driving dream of any teenager at that time.

Frank flipped me the keys, said "Happy birthday, kid", and invited me in.

I just stood there staring.

"Uh…are you saying I can drive the car for a while?"

"Drive it for as long as you want. It's yours."

"Mine? To keep?"

"Yeah. Now come inside."

And, with that, I knew that I owned the car. It was also clear that there was to be no more conversation about it with Frank. As I came to learn, when Frank had said or done what he set out to say or do, that was it. Case closed. On to the next.

Following Frank inside, I first met Jilly Rizzo, Frank's bodyguard, companion, and future restaurateur. Even though I wasn't totally sure at the time who Damon Runyan was, I remember that Jilly immediately struck me as the quintessential Runyanesque character. He was thickset and seemed more like a human version of Ferdinand the Bull than a real person. His hellos, yeses, and most other responses were accomplished with a unique grunt, one that I would grow to love and anticipate. He also had a wandering eye, so you were never quite sure if he was looking directly at you or not. Depending on how he felt about you that could have been a very good thing. At that time, I had no idea who he was or what he did for Frank. I simply had the instinctive feeling that I should probably always keep on Jilly's good side, assuming I could figure out what side that was.

We sat down and Frank explained to me that my father, quite simply, had saved his career.

I already knew that Sinatra had been a huge star in the 1930s and

1940s as a singer, a teen idol, and in movies. He told me that he had, however, suffered some health problems and that his film career had "gone into the toilet." I found out later that he had actually hemorrhaged his vocal chords twice in 1949 and 1950 and that the 1948 movie *The Kissing Bandit* had been a disaster for him.

In 1951, my Dad, who had been a huge Sinatra fan, had called Frank to his office at Columbia to tell him that the studio had purchased the film rights to *From Here To Eternity*, a soon-to-be bestselling book. Dad told Sinatra that there was a character in the film named Maggio that would be perfect for Sinatra and promised Sinatra the part.

I later discovered that Columbia had purchased the rights to the book from its author James Jones in March 1951 for eighty-five thousand dollars.

My sister Susie told me that Jones was our constant houseguest during that period of time. She remembers Dad having the manuscript for the book, not the book itself. Susie was twelve at the time and wanted to read the manuscript too and Dad would let her read certain passages but only after he had "crossed out a lot of the bad words."

Frank told me that he immediately read the book and was fascinated by the character of Maggio. He called my Dad to say he was "in."

Frank then said that Dad called Sinatra a few days later to say that Harry Cohn had overruled him. My father profusely apologized to Sinatra and told him that he had resigned from the studio in protest.

"Your Dad was a stand-up guy, Stephen. You need to know that. He really put his ass on the line for me."

Frank did not tell me the details of what happened next, except to say that Harry Cohn changed his mind and that Frank got the role. Red Skelton and Ray Stark would later fill in the missing details for me.

Sinatra won the 1953 Academy Award for Best Supporting Actor for playing Maggio and *From Here To Eternity* became the most lucrative movie that Columbia had made to date.

"That part changed everything for me, Stephen," Frank said. "After Maggio, people took me seriously as an actor. Without your Dad, that might have never happened."

Frank then explained that my father's sudden death (May 17, 1951) within a couple of months after the incident with Cohn, and long before production had even begun on the film, had prevented Frank from being able to repay my Dad.

That's where I came in.

Frank told me that he felt that he could only repay my father through his son so he had transferred his gratitude from my father to me. That certainly explained all the great gifts, culminating in that amazing Corvette out in the driveway.

Frank was not very close at that time with his own son. It's really eerie for me when I look at my relationships with Sinatra, Ronald Reagan, Ray Stark, and Dino De Laurentiis, all of whom had sons who had either tragically died or from whom they were estranged.

My Dad had died, I was not close with my stepfather, and these amazing men appeared in my life. Obviously, I benefited hugely from that transference.

Frank introduced me to Dorothy, his private secretary, and gave me a little business card with a private phone number on it. He told me that, by calling that number, I would always be able to connect with someone who could immediately reach him. Dorothy told me that she or someone else would update the number when it changed. For years to come, that is exactly what happened.

"Stephen, I know you're a good kid but even good kids from Beverly Hills get into trouble."

He then stared really hard at me, in an intense way that I had never experienced before. "If you ever, and I mean, ever, get into any kind of real trouble, you have to call me."

He then leaned back a bit and said "I want you to see me as a kind of godfather. I need to be the one you call if the shit hits the fan."

I was somewhat taken aback by his insistence, but I was also wildly flattered, honored, and thrilled that Frank Sinatra was going to look out for me. I remember feeling an invulnerable rush of adrenaline and blurted out "Yes, sir, absolutely. I promise."

He then said "We're going to have some fun together, you and I. Meet me tonight at The Daisy."

The Daisy was the club at that time in Beverly Hills. It also had the dubious distinction years later of being the club where O.J. Simpson met his future wife Nicole.

Frank then gave me one of those patented Sinatra winks, we shook hands, and I raced off in my new Corvette.

Later that night, I met Frank briefly at The Daisy where he introduced me to the people at the door, the security guys, and anyone else he could find. He let it be known that I was family and that "Stephen" should be treated as such any time I wanted to come in.

Frank, who had a certain formality about him, was the first person in my life ever to call me Stephen, rather than Steve, and I grew to love being referred to by my whole name.

Frank didn't stay long that night and I felt a bit awkward and uncomfortable there without him, so my stay was brief, too, and I headed back up Beverly Drive for the brief trip to my parents' home.

That was one of the great birthdays of my life.

I was totally stoked (yes, it was that era) that I had entered the nightlife of Sinatra's world and that I had the ultimate get-out- of jail-free card from The Chairman of the Board.

I felt utterly invincible, never really believing that I would ever actually call on Sinatra for that kind of assistance.

After all, as Frank had said, I was a nice Jewish kid from Beverly Hills. How could I ever get into that kind of trouble?

I had no idea that, only a few years later, I would desperately need Frank's help.

For the time being, however, I was eighteen years old, and Frank Sinatra had decided that I should have some adult fun. That was, as my stepfather was fond of saying, a hell of a lot better than being poked in the groin with an oyster fork.

That encounter with Frank in the summer of 1964 was the beginning of a fascinating five-year period with my "godfather."

Being Sent Away

A couple of weeks after receiving that Corvette, I met Steve Renzin, who lived in Philadelphia. Steve and three friends were driving around the country to celebrate their high school graduation.

I quickly learned that Steve was going to attend Penn in the fall. After having lost another personality clash with my stepfather, so was I. For years, my stepfather and I had been at odds, so much so that I had been sent away in 1962 for my last two years of high school to a strict boy's boarding school in Northern California.

While I hated both the school and being sent away from my friends, I did meet a friend there who would have a rather illustrious future.

The guy who lived three doors down from my little cubicle was a flamenco guitarist par excellence. His one desire was to become the next Sabicas, who was then the most famous flamenco guitarist in the world. My classmate hated rock music. Which is why I was more than shocked just a few years later when I saw him on *The Ed Sullivan Show*.

My old schoolmate Robbie Krieger had become the guitarist for The Doors and actually wrote "Light My Fire."

After graduating from Menlo, I was looking forward to going to school in Philadelphia about as much as I would have looked forward to an arm-wrestling match with Jilly Rizzo.

After all, it was 1964. The Beatles had just electrified our entire generation with a whole new sound in music, the free speech movement was a-borning in Berkeley with Mario Savio and Angela Davis, free love was everywhere, marijuana was the drug of choice, I had a new Corvette, Frank Sinatra had invited me out to play…and I was going to Philadelphia?

(To the fine folks in Philly: in my later and brief incarnation as a lawyer/sports agent, I did get Ron Jaworski traded from the Los Angeles Rams to the Philadelphia Eagles and Ron did lead them to the Super Bowl, so I hope that gets me a bit off the hook?)

When Steve Renzin and I realized we were going to be classmates, and he discovered how much I was dreading the move to Philadelphia, we became fast friends, and have remained so ever since. Back in the day, Steve shared many of my adventures with Sinatra. Today, Steve is a very successful gynecologist in New Rochelle, New York.

"I'm With Sinatra!"

Steve came home from Philadelphia with me for Christmas break in 1964 and had his first close encounter with my godfather.

Steve, my friend Jim Wiatt, and I were at the famed Whisky-a-Go-Go on the Sunset Strip. This was before they removed the "y" and made it Whisk-a-Go-Go, a move that always made as much sense to me as Prince changing his name to a symbol.

Jim Wiatt and I had met on our first day at Beverly Hills High School in 1960 and had been close friends ever since. We later worked together in politics for California Senator John Tunney, and even entered the film business at the same time, me with Ray Stark, and Jim with an agent named Frank Cooper. (Later, Jim would become the Chief Executive Officer of The William Morris Agency.)

While at the Whisky, Jim, Steve, and I met three girls from Michigan who were in L.A. for the upcoming 1965 New Year's Day Rose Bowl game between Michigan and Oregon.

The girls wanted to try to meet celebrities, and we wanted to impress the girls. I suggested we go to The Daisy, where, assuming that someone would remember me from my time there with Sinatra six months earlier, I thought I could get us in. The girls were thrilled, if a little suspicious, and we all caravanned down Sunset to The Daisy on Rodeo Drive just north of Wilshire in Beverly Hills.

Back then, Rodeo Drive was nothing like the international shopping Mecca that it is today. It was much quieter, sleepy even. More like the back street to Beverly Drive, just one block to the east, where places like Nate 'n Al's Delicatessen and the real Beverly Hills existed.

Franks' clothier of choice, Carroll and Co., was a couple of blocks up the street from the Daisy on the corner of Rodeo and Little Santa Monica Blvd. The other notable place on Rodeo at that time was just up and across the street from The Daisy. Replete with Tiki torches lighting a bridge over a little lagoon at the entrance to a dimly lit restaurant, the wonderfully exotic Polynesian restaurant called The Luau also became famous as a safe haven for clandestine Hollywood affairs.

When we arrived at The Daisy, the club was packed and there was a line out the door. Leaving my companions behind me, and trying to act as though I owned the place, I sauntered up to the door in hopes that someone would remember me.

No such luck. I was met with blank stares and an "Oh, sure, we've heard that line before" attitude. Until one security guy said, "Oh, yeah, Sinatra, right?"

"Yes. Frank Sinatra. He said someone would always let me in."

With that, he responded. "Mr. Sinatra just happens to be here tonight, kid. And he doesn't like people he's never met using his name. Unless you want me to go get him and have him tell us to throw you out, I suggest you get your butt out of here now."

Knowing that he thought I would make a mad dash into the night, I stood my ground. I wasn't sure if he was bluffing to see if I was bluffing, or if Frank was really there, but I decided there was nothing to lose and stared the guy down.

"Oh, he's here. Great. Tell him Stephen Deutsch is here. And don't tell him you kept me waiting. He probably wouldn't take that very well."

A long moment hung in the air and then it was Mr. Security's turn to look a little nervous.

Instead of going to find Frank, he took me by the arm and we headed into the Daisy. He probably didn't have the nerve to call Frank to the door or he still thought I was bluffing.

In any case, we walked into the club.

And there was Frank with Jilly.

I hadn't seen him since I left for college four months earlier. When he saw me, he brightened and yelled out "Hey, Stephen, get on over here."

With that, I thought my security escort might just pass out. Blanching, he quickly whispered to me "Hey, please don't tell Mr. Sinatra I tried to stop you. I need this job, man." I told him to forget it and asked him to please go get my friends outside, which he rushed to do.

I was never questioned about getting into The Daisy again.

While my newfound-best-friend-security-guard was gone, Frank asked how school was and what I was doing there. I just managed to get out a brief explanation when Steve, Jim, and the three Wolverine women were ushered in.

Frank jumped into action.

He shook hands with everyone and, of course, the girls were struck speechless. He got us a table and sat down with us to talk. Steve remembers he was there for almost thirty minutes. I think it was more like ten; however, the result was the same. The girls were star struck and totally enchanted.

At one point, the girls got up en masse to go to the bathroom, giggling to each other as they left.

Before I could even say thank you, Frank got up, and leaned into the three of us. "If you guys don't have sex tonight, you never will."

Another Sinatra wink, and he was gone.

And I was supposed to go back to cheese steak in Philadelphia?

But go back I did until I moved home again in early 1966, the year that Frank married Mia Farrow.

This is a good moment for me to clarify something about my relationship with Frank.

I was neither Frank's confidante nor his friend. To Frank, I was Sylvan Simon's son, and I was very clear on, grateful for, and proud of that identity. Other than that brief moment around my eighteenth birthday, Frank didn't discuss either his personal or professional life with me. The discussions were almost always either about me or about politics or sports or something like that. I never would have presumed to ask him a personal question and he did not open up that area of his life to me.

I turned twenty-one in 1967 and received a great birthday call from Frank, telling me that he wanted me to come to Palm Springs, but he then kind of disappeared for a while and the visit didn't actually happen until 1968.

Doing Vegas with The Chairman of the Board

My friends and I would often take what was then a three-hour drive from Beverly Hills to Palm Springs. "The Springs" was the same vacation magnet to kids from L.A. as Fort Lauderdale is and was to young people from the East.

When I did see Frank in Palm Springs in 1968, he introduced me to Danny Schwartz, one of Frank's business associates. Danny had made a fortune in the billboard business and, along with his wife Natalie, owned a house not too far from Frank. Danny also owned some racehorses and quickly discovered that I had a love for the track as well. (Incidentally, Danny's horse trainer at that time was Monty Roberts, the real-life horse whisperer.)

Danny knew of my relationship with Frank, and he offered me a part-time job, the details of which are so obscure in my mind that I don't think it amounted to much more than traveling around with and hanging out with Danny. A lot of the time, that meant being in Vegas with Danny and Frank.

Tough duty, but somebody had to do it.

Traveling to Vegas with the Sinatra entourage provided quite a high for a young man and, even though I enjoyed that benefit only a few times, the feeling is forever etched in my memory.

I enjoyed red carpet treatment everywhere and high-end accommodations at Caesar's Palace, where everything was on the house.

I was allowed to sit in with Frank and Danny while they played Baccarat for the table limit (three thousand dollars sticks in my mind, but that may be off) every hand.

I also fondly remember going to Frank's shows and also seeing Sammy Davis, Jr. and Dean Martin perform.

Heady stuff indeed.

The overriding feeling was, however, pride and awe. Just hanging out with Frank Sinatra was a heady experience. His charisma was so off the charts that it felt like there was a change in air density when he entered a room.

I also adored Jilly Rizzo. Yes, I know now of the tough reputation he had but, with me, he was always a great practical joker, protector, and racetrack companion.

Jilly was also my guide through the maze of Las Vegas and I was still pretty naïve about certain things. One night, I told Jilly that it was really weird that every time we were at Caesar's Palace with Frank, there was some princess who was also always there. I thought maybe she was a huge Sinatra fan. Jilly asked me what the hell I was talking about.

"Every time we're in the casino, I hear them paging Princess Fatima, Jilly."

Jilly just gave me this great deadpan look and said, "That's the code they use for the hookers, Stephen."

Aaaah, Vegas.

Someone else told me later that Jilly was just pulling my leg, and that Fatima was actually the code the pit bosses used for calling cigarette girls.

On another occasion, Jilly and I agreed to fly with one of Danny Schwartz's racehorses from L.A. to New York for a stakes race at Aqueduct.

At that time, cargo planes that carried horses only left LAX at night and flew redeye flights to New York. Jilly and I arrived with the horse and we put him on a huge empty cargo plane, with two seats for ourselves. We wondered aloud why the plane was so empty except for the horses and us, when dozens of hearses began to pull up to the plane. Turns out that the rest of the cargo was coffins, some of which carried soldiers who had died in Vietnam.

We rode all night with the horse and the coffins. That was a ride I never forgot, but never discussed with Jilly again.

So, that's how it went in 1968 with Frank. Going to Vegas and Palm Springs. Occasionally seeing Frank at my parents' house.

On a couple of other occasions, I was also invited to join Frank for Sunday night dinner at Matteo's, owned by the ubiquitous Matty Jordan.

Matteo's' was the hangout for Frank, his pals, and many other stars in the 1960s and 1970s.

Unlike some of the other "in" restaurants and clubs of those days, like The Luau, Romanoff's, Don the Beachcomber, The Cocoanut Grove, and Chasen's, all of which I also frequented with my parents, Matteo's is still operating in its original Westwood Blvd. location to this very day.

Matteo (Matty) Jordan was such a wonderful character that he could have later been cast in *The Sopranos*. Even then, you'd think he was over the top, but that was Matty, the irrepressible Italian host whose portrait of himself as General George Patton still hangs in the restaurant today. Matty named dishes like Steak Sinatra after the actors and other personalities who put Matteo's on the map.

As a result of my relationship with Sinatra, Matty took particular care to make me feel welcome, especially when I came in with my friends, or a date. He always made it clear to anyone who was with me that I was an important patron. Obviously, I was in no way an important client and he didn't have to do that but that was his way. He was warm, funny, and charming, the perfect host.

And that brings us to 1969, the year that everything changed, both in my life, and in my relationship with Frank.

Two Showgirls: "Frank Sent Us." "Frank Who?"

Steve Renzin and I had remained friends after I left Philadelphia. When Steve graduated Penn in 1968, he entered medical school at Wayne State in Detroit in the fall and a few months later came out to visit me.

While Steve was staying with me, Frank's secretary called me to say that Frank was inviting me to come to Palm Springs and fly with him and Danny Schwartz to Vegas for a party. When I told her about Steve being with me and that Frank knew Steve from The Daisy encounter and other times when Steve was visiting, she said she would check with Frank about bringing Steve along. She quickly called me back to confirm that Frank said it would be fine.

Steve really wanted to go to Vegas, but he had not brought along the appropriate clothing. When Frank heard about that, he told us to go to Carroll and Company on Rodeo Drive, get some things for Steve, and that Frank would have them put the clothes on his account.

Steve was flabbergasted that Frank would do that. Frank also gave Steve a pair of cuff links as a gift that Steve treasured for years. That was the kind of gracious and generous thing Frank Sinatra constantly did for his friends, and, in this case, the friend of a friend.

We drove down to Palm Springs and flew on Frank's jet with Frank, Nancy, Jr., and Tina to Las Vegas.

Steve and I shared a room at Caesar's and loved the freedom of finally being over twenty-one so we could gamble with the "big guys."

One night, Frank introduced us to Sammy Davis, Jr.

When Steve mentioned that he was in medical school in Detroit,

Sammy told Steve that he would be performing in Detroit soon and gave Steve a number to call so Steve could come to the concert and bring some of his medical school friends. Steve was thrilled and asked how many people he could actually bring. Sammy responded by telling him he could count on ten or fifteen tickets. Sammy later came through, too, and Steve became a hero to his classmates.

The next night, Frank got us great seats for a show at Caesar's that featured some incredibly beautiful showgirls. During the show, Frank came up to us and told us that we should each pick out two showgirls and that they would meet us in our room later that night.

At first, we thought he was kidding, but, when he gave us an exact time when they would arrive at our room, we quickly realized that he was dead serious. Wanting desperately to be seen as two of the guys, we both jumped in, pointed out two girls each, and thanked Frank profusely.

It's important to note here that we were both twenty-two and wanted to believe that we could handle anything. We also wanted each other to believe that we could handle anything. As close as we were as friends, we didn't want to admit to each other that the idea of being in bed with two Vegas showgirls each actually terrified both of us out of our wits.

Performance anxiety with performers might be an apt description of how we were both feeling, but there was no way that either of us would be the first to express our fears to the other. Male ego, the eternal bane of our existence, ruled once again.

So, to build up our fortitude and try to drive the fear away, we drank a little, and then more than a little.

Finally, the appointed time arrived and we went to our room.

And we waited, staring at each other.

Finally, there was a knock at the door.

Neither of us moved.

There was another knock, this time accompanied by a woman's voice calling our name. As were both named Steve, that wasn't difficult to discern.

Another knock was followed by a very feminine "Frank sent us."

The moment of truth had arrived.

And we completely chickened out.

With panic in our eyes, we looked at each other and simultaneously whispered, "Don't say anything!"

There was one more knock at the door and then silence.

After a few moments, we looked at each other and dissolved in laughter, falling to the floor.

"You are such a coward," Steve taunted me.

"No way! You were much more scared than I was."

"You're pathetic. The only reason I didn't answer the door is because I knew you were so scared."

"Oh, right. I thought you were going to pee your pants so I didn't want to embarrass you."

And so it has gone now for the last forty years.

Truth be told, we were both way too nervous to have sex with a Vegas showgirl, let alone two of them, let alone with the other one of us in the next bed. What if one of us had failed to perform and the other hadn't? That scar would have been permanent.

Simply put, we were inexperienced, frightened kids.

There are two postscripts to that sorry night.

First, Frank didn't say a word to either one of us about it. We knew that his silence could have been interpreted in two ways. He either knew that we had chickened out and didn't want to embarrass us, or the girls never told him that their mission was unsuccessful and he assumed we had done our manly duty.

We preferred the second scenario but were pretty sure that the first scenario was more likely, a fact which Frank later confirmed to me when I finally got into that real trouble that we had talked about on my eighteenth birthday.

The second and more mortifying postscript is that Frank did exactly the same thing, many years later in Houston, Texas, with my nephew Don Granger. Don, who was single at the time, welcomed the girl into his room with glee and open arms.

At one time in Don's youth, I was his idol.

How the mighty have fallen.

A brief note on Don and life imitating art, imitating life: At the age of sixteen, Don visited me while we were shooting *Somewhere in Time* on Mackinac Island in the summer of 1979. Much to the chagrin and displeasure of his neurologist father, Don became utterly enamored of the film business. A five-day visit extended to several weeks and Don logged several appearances as an extra in the film. Don also worked at other odd jobs on the set, and that was it.

Don was hooked. Even though he honored his father, and worked for a time on Wall Street, his heart was already in the film business.

While I was producing *She's Out of Control* in 1988 for the Weintraub Company, Don got a job there and his career rocketed off into the stratosphere, far eclipsing mine.

After a successful stint at Disney, he became Executive Vice-President at Paramount where he supervised countless successful films, such as *Saving Private Ryan*, *Clear and Present Danger*, and *Mission: Impossible*.

For several years after Paramount, Don was the head of Cruise/Wagner Productions, the production company owned by Tom Cruise, with whom I worked twenty-five years ago. Six degrees of separation indeed.

He later became the President of United Artists, and is now an independent producer, a loving husband to Lisa McRee (the former host of *Good Morning, America*), and an amazing father of two great kids.

Godfather....Help!!!

The next time I went to Vegas, which was very soon after the adventure there with Steve, would turn out to be the fateful moment when I had to frantically turn to Frank for his help.

We were at Caesar's Palace for the closing night of one of Frank's engagements. Frank was scheduled to fly back to Palm Springs in his plane right after the performance but I decided to stay on.

Truth is, I had become enamored of someone else's wife. She was in Vegas without her well-known husband, and I was utterly bedazzled by her. She was a couple of years older than me, gorgeous, and sexy. She also made it very clear to me that she was available and interested.

After Frank's performance, which I attended with the lady in question, he indeed left for the airport and we went directly to her suite. It was a very passionate encounter and, very quickly, we were naked in bed, with our clothes strewn about the floor.

Looking back on that night, I'm amazed that I actually took that chance with her. Not because she was married, a fact which I conveniently rationalized away when she told me that she and her husband had a very open marriage and understood that each would stray off the reservation from time to time. This was the 1960s and that at least allowed me to pretend that I wasn't doing anything wrong.

No, it wasn't that. The truth was that, before that night, I had only had sex with two other women. I was, in fact, pretty damn inexperienced but I was determined not to be intimidated again. Yes, I know. The male ego. Be it ever so humblingly pathetic, there's no place like hormones.

I had chickened out before in my life, and not just with those showgirls.

Two of my mother and stepfather's close friends were Freddie and Janet deCordova. Freddie was the producer of *The Tonight Show* with Johnny Carson. His wife Janet was an attractive, vivacious woman in her forties who so openly flirted with me that, after *The Graduate* was released, she sent me a photograph of her.

Clad only in a mink coat, she signed it: " To Benjamin…Love, Mrs. Robinson."

Like the on-screen Benjamin, I was terrified.

Unlike the on-screen Benjamin, nothing ever happened with Janet.

So, on that night in Vegas with a different woman, I was determined to face my fears.

As we began to make love, and I mean we had just begun, we heard the hallway door to the living room of the suite open, and her husband yell out "Surprise, I'm here!"

Surprise?

More like blood stopping, paralytic "oh-shit-I'm-a dead-man-who-is going-to-hell-right-now!"

"You have to get out of here. He'll kill you," she hissed at me.

As I had already entertained that particular thought at least ten times in the previous two seconds, along with visions of how painful and drawn out my death might be, I didn't need a second warning.

If there had been an Olympic Event in underwear donning, I would have been the Gold Medalist.

With only my underwear on, and the rest of my clothes in my arms, I bolted out of the bedroom door of the suite and raced down the hall in the opposite direction of the living room of the suite.

Thank God I somehow had the presence of mind to go to the stairs, not the elevator. As I entered the stairwell, I heard a man's voice shout out for me to stop but I was fairly sure he hadn't actually seen me. I raced down the stairs, hurriedly putting on my clothes as I went.

Fortunately, I knew Caesar's very well by that time so I ran to an area where I prayed that I would still find Jilly whom I knew had not gone on the plane with Frank.

Prayers answered, Jilly was indeed still there.

I raced up and grabbed him, which, in retrospect, exposed me to vastly more potential danger than being caught by my pursuer.

Jilly reflexively reached for a gun that he often had on him, grabbed me by the shirt, and asked me what the hell was wrong?

Now terrified and realizing that I had at least two people who might want to kill me, I blurted out what had just happened and begged him to protect me.

There was a brief pause, in which I thought Jilly was going to hit me.

While I was wondering which hospital they would take me to for the broken face I was about to experience, Jilly burst out laughing. A huge, gut-level, belly laugh, not some chuckle or guffaw. His face got so red that I thought he might pass out, if I didn't beat him to it.

Recovering, he gave me a bear hug, put his arm around my shoulder, and ushered me into a private office where he picked up a phone and started dialing.

"Frank's gotta hear this. Right now."

"But he just flew back home. He'll…"

"…kill us both if we don't tell him right now," Jilly responded. "And I ain't dying 'cause you couldn't keep your pants on."

Jilly reached Frank at his home in Palm Springs.

All he said to Frank was "Frank, the kid's got something to tell ya." And then he handed me the phone.

When I explained what had happened to Frank, he too roared with laughter.

I thought maybe Ralph Edwards was going to pop up and tell me *This is Your Life* or that Allen Funt was going to appear from behind a *Candid Camera*. What the hell was so funny about me being scared out of my mind, with an irate husband on my tail who was dedicated, I was sure, to castrating me with a dull butter knife from room service?

Jilly saw the look on my face and whispered, "Is he cracking up, too?" When I nodded yes, I realized that both Jilly and Frank were actually very proud of me for getting myself in the situation. Frank was also thrilled that I had finally called on my godfather for his protection.

"I told you you'd need me one day, kid. Give the phone back to Jilly. Oh, and by the way, congratulations for not chickening out this time."

Great, I was scared to death and I just got confirmation of the fact that Frank knew that Steve and I had chickened out with the showgirls. Was I ever going to wake up from this nightmare or was Rod Serling going to walk in and welcome me to my own private *Twilight Zone*?

Jilly grabbed the phone, shared another laugh with Frank, did a couple of his patented grunts and an "OK, got it" into the phone, and hung up.

Jilly then told me that Frank was on his way back to his plane to fly back to Vegas. I was stunned. He had just flown back to Palm Springs a couple of hours before.

"What's he going to do?" I asked.

"He'll figure that out on the plane. C'mon. Let's go."

Frightened again, I asked where we were going.

"Oh, I dunno. Maybe we can play blackjack for a couple of hours," Jilly responded.

Now I knew I was a dead man walking.

"Are you kidding me?" I blurted out.

Even with my reduced mental capacity at that moment, I knew better than to ever ask Jilly if he was crazy.

Jilly just laughed and said he was actually taking me to his room to wait for Frank. After Jilly let me in, he told me to rest for a while and not to leave the room, no matter what. As if I was going to even stick my head out in the hall. Right.

"Take a nap," he said.

"A nap," I thought. I was sure I wouldn't sleep for at least a week, and even then, it would be with one eye open and with the biggest shotgun I could find on my lap.

To my great shock, though, I did actually doze off for a while.

About three hours later, I was awakened with a start as Jilly walked in with Frank, who was beaming from ear to ear.

"Frank, I'm so sorry. So sorry. Can you really help me with this?" I asked.

"Already taken care of. C'mon, let's go home."

Already taken care of? Even though I was a little nervous to ask, I wanted to know if I would always have to look over my shoulder if I ever came back to Vegas again. Or, for that matter, anywhere else.

Frank explained to me that, as soon as he had arrived, he and Jilly went to see my pursuer. I swallowed a bit hard on that one.

"Then what happened?" I asked Frank.

Frank winked at Jilly and Jilly simply said:

"Frank made him an offer he couldn't refuse."

Mystified, I asked what that meant, but Frank just laughed and said, "Don't worry about it. It's over. Come on, you're coming back to The Springs with me."

The novel of *The Godfather* was published that very year, but I didn't read it, so the impact of Frank's comment was completely lost on me until I saw *The Godfather* film when it was released in 1972. More on the eeriness of that connection a bit later in this chapter.

Jilly had gathered my things from my room and we headed to the airport to fly back to Palm Springs on Frank's plane.

I felt an immense sense of relief when the wheels actually lifted off the ground, and I remember making a promise to myself that I would never go back to Vegas. Ever. As with most promises like that, I broke it much sooner than I ever thought I would.

On the plane, Frank and Jilly had a grand old time teasing me and asking me every intimate question they could possibly concoct about my brief bed encounter. For all the fear and trouble it caused, the episode had indeed been awfully brief and utterly unconsummated.

I told Frank that I was never going back to Vegas and he just laughed.

"Sure, you will. I told you that you're safe and you are. You were right. He didn't actually see you, so he has no idea who you are, just that you're a friend of mine, he's a friend of mine, and that's good enough."

"He's a friend of yours?"

"Well, not a close friend but we know each other and he's actually a pretty decent guy. Anyway, it's not like it's the first time this has happened with the two of them."

I then decided to just shut up and be grateful that Frank had come to my aid when I needed him. He was also so genuinely elated that he had been given the chance to fulfill a promise that he had made to himself that I felt touched and happy, too.

We arrived in Palm Springs and went to Frank's house. I was ushered into a guest room. Frank gave me a gentle and loving pat on the face and told me he was proud of me.

I think that was the closest I ever came to getting a hug from Frank.

I then collapsed on the bed and fell into the deepest and most relieved sleep that I had ever experienced.

Red Skelton Fills In The Blanks

In some ways, that Vegas moment with Frank signaled a change in our relationship. Frank had more than fulfilled his promise both to me and to the memory of my Dad.

In Palm Springs later in 1969, I had an encounter that filled in the missing pieces of the Harry Cohn saga.

During that trip, I was leaving a movie theater one night and noticed that Red Skelton and his wife Georgia were walking out, too.

Even though I was a huge fan of his television show, I had not seen him in person since I was about four years old. Although I was sure he wouldn't recognize me, I was nevertheless drawn to say hello to him.

I walked up to him and started by saying "Excuse me, Mr. Skelton, you won't remember me but…"

At that point, he looked right at me and exclaimed, "Oh my God, you're Sylvan's boy!"

"Uncle" Red hadn't seen me since I was a child but, as he explained when we sat down at a nearby coffee shop, I looked so much like my Dad that he knew me instantly.

For the next hour or so, often with a choked-up voice and tears running down his cheeks, Red Skelton talked to me about my Dad.

How much he loved Dad, how much he depended on him to direct his films and, most importantly, how much he loved him as a man. Over and over, he explained how warm and friendly Dad was to everyone. How much he loved people, how easily he laughed, and how much he loved both my sister and me.

I will never forget that evening with Red because, more than any other conversation I have ever had with anyone, before or since, he made my Dad come alive for me.

Red missed him so much, loved him so much, and was so passionate in his expression of his love, that I could actually feel my Dad's presence.

So, there we were, both of us crying, with Georgia holding Red's hand.

As fate would have it, there was even a more serendipitous reason for me to have run into Red that night.

At one point in the conversation, Red asked me how often I came down to Palm Springs. When I told him about my relationship with Frank and what Frank had said about his gratitude to my Dad, the last veils were about to be lifted from what had really happened so many years before.

I was about to find out how Dad had really died and what had really happened with Frank Sinatra and Harry Cohn.

As I was then in my early twenties, Red quite innocently and understandably assumed that I knew the truth about Dad's death, so he offhandedly mentioned how devastated he was about Dad's addiction to Gynergin and how tragic the brain hemorrhage had been.

Gynergin. Hemorrhage. Say what?

I never could have made it as an actor and I have always been a supremely lousy poker player, so there was no way for me to hide my shock at what I was hearing.

Georgia noted it first and I saw her squeeze Red's hand to get his attention. He saw the expression on my face as well and then it was his turn to look stricken. He knew, however, that he couldn't withdraw what he had just said.

I told him the cover story that my mother had told for years. Dad had died of a heart attack because he worked too hard.

Red was incredulous.

"Didn't that make you worry about working too hard in your own life?" he asked.

Bingo.

Red then told me that Dad suffered from crippling migraine headaches. A doctor had given him a drug called Gynergin, which he could inject when the headaches came. Evidently, Dad had accidentally overdosed and died almost instantly from a cerebral hemorrhage.

I felt the emotional equivalent of having instantaneously aligned all the squares in a Rubik's cube. If there had been a dictionary definition of "world class underachiever" at that time, it should have read "See Stephen Deutsch."

I realized how terrified I had been of working on anything so extensively that it would kill me, as work had supposedly killed my father.

There was a sudden rush of liberating energy in my whole being in that moment. I also had the palpable feeling of my Dad's spirit there at the table, saying "Thank you, pal" to Red.

I thanked Red profusely for his honesty and told him how wonderful I felt. I also told him that I had to go talk to my mother about why she hadn't ever told me the truth, even after almost twenty years. As he seemed completely unfazed by the prospect of having been the one to reveal the truth to me, I got the distinct sense that Red was not terribly fond of my mother.

Then things got really interesting.

Red leaned in and said, "Well, as this seems to be a night for telling the truth, just how much of the story did Sinatra really tell you?"

I told him everything Frank had told me.

With a glance at Georgia, he said that everything Frank had told me was the truth, but there were details that had been left out. He said he was going to tell me the story as my father had related it to him. He also cautioned me that it would not be a great idea to ask Sinatra himself to confirm the details.

I still remember the hairs standing up on the back of my neck as he started to fill in the blanks.

"Your Dad was a huge Sinatra fan. Huge. So when he read *From Here To Eternity*, he immediately thought of Sinatra for Maggio and called him just the way Sinatra explained it to you. When your Dad told Harry Cohn, he went nuts. Cohn hated Sinatra, mostly because of some girl Harry wanted who had an affair with Sinatra instead. So Harry overruled your Dad. Sylvan was a man of his word, Steve, and he told Cohn that he would have to leave the studio if he couldn't keep his word. Cohn said, 'Fine, leave.' Your Dad called Sinatra and left the studio.

"A few days later, Cohn called your Dad and told him to come back and give Sinatra the part."

"Your Dad was shocked because Cohn never did that sort of thing and it took a while for anyone to figure out what had happened."

"Turns out Harry owned a piece of a racehorse named Ponder or Yonder or something like that. The horse was poisoned in its stall and a note was shoved under the door at Cohn's house, saying 'You're next.' Somebody said they got into the house and put it under Harry's bedroom door and other people said it was the front door. Anyway, that's when Harry called your Dad."

"Sylvan never brought it up to Sinatra so I have no idea if Sinatra knew anything about it until after the fact when we all found out."

I was utterly mesmerized by Red's story.

We talked a bit more but finally, it was time to go.

As we were about to go our separate ways that night, Red gave me a huge bear hug and told me that he expected me to always act in a way that would make my Dad proud of me.

I promised him that I would do my best.

"You're your father's son. That'll be good enough."

With that, he walked off into the Palm Springs night.

I never saw him again.

The Queen of Denial

On my drive back to L.A., I decided that Red was absolutely right and that I shouldn't say anything to Frank.

As I have previously mentioned, conversations with Frank after my eighteenth birthday were almost never about him.

As it pertained to Frank, whatever happened back in 1951 was none of my business and I wasn't going to question my benefactor.

I also need to say here that no one ever told me that Frank knew about what happened to Cohn's horse until long after it had happened. I also later learned that Frank really hated the fact that so many people just assumed that the Johnny Fontane character in the film of *The Godfather* was factually based on his experiences.

I did, however, want to ask both my mother and Ray Stark if Dad had told them the same story that Red had told me, or if either of them had any independent knowledge of what had happened.

Talking to my mother about my father had never been easy.

Even though she always told me that I should ask her anything about him that I wanted to know, her actions on the few times when I did broach the subject with her quickly discouraged me from mentioning Dad around her.

She had always become very emotional and would quickly start to cry. She also would act very concerned that my stepfather would hear or know we were talking about Dad because she was convinced that he would become hurt or offended if he knew I was talking about my father.

This time, though, I told her that we had to talk and that she really needed to hang in there with me and not walk away in tears.

I first told her what Red had told me about the circumstances surrounding Dad's death.

Her initial response was to vehemently deny Red's explanation of how Dad had died, but Red had been way too adamant and detailed in his explanation for me to just let it go that easily. I explained to Mom what a profound effect her explanation had caused in my own life, particularly with my work ethic. I was also a man, or claimed to be anyway, and I beseeched my mother to respect both me and the memory of my father and tell me what I deserved to know. The truth.

For a flicker of a second, she hesitated.

And I knew immediately that Red had been right.

It was only then that Mom corroborated Red's story about Dad's drug use. In a torrent, the whole saga came rushing out of her.

Dad was a workaholic and Cohn was a stern taskmaster. She also told me that she was so worried about Dad's headaches that she had actually asked Harry Cohn to fire my father and that Cohn had refused.

She added to Red's famous quote about Harry Cohn's funeral with her own opinion that the only sad thing about Cohn's death was that it had been painless.

She also reminded me that it had been Cohn who had given me that shot of whiskey when I was four years old.

Interestingly enough, Mom's sentiments about Harry Cohn did not extend to his widow Joan, with whom she was still quite friendly. Cohn's son Harrison was actually a playmate of mine when I was younger and, even after Mom's remarriage, I spent time at the Cohn estate on Lexington Drive in Beverly Hills, just north of the Beverly Hills Hotel. I remember fondly that Harrison and his brother John had an entire room that was completely filled with an electric train set.

Joan Cohn later married the actor Laurence Harvey and they were frequent guests in my stepfather's home.

When we got to the Sinatra story, I told Mom what Red had explained to me, and Mom became very agitated.

She vehemently blurted out "that old fool Red should have kept his mouth shut."

I never did discover what had gone sour between my mother and Red Skelton, but it was obvious that something had poisoned the relationship between them.

Mom was very concerned that I would say something to Frank or anyone else for that matter. She had remained close with Frank as well and didn't want to do anything to upset or offend him.

I assured her that I had no intention of talking to Frank about it. For me, this whole thing was a major link to my father, not about Sinatra himself, but Mom absolutely refused to discuss Sinatra in any way.

It was interesting to me that she didn't deny anything. She just seemed terrified that I would approach Sinatra with any of what I had been told. She had opened up about Dad's death but erected a stone wall around any Sinatra discussion.

Dad's Protégé

The next day, I called Ray Stark and told him I needed to talk to him about my Dad. We set up a time for me to go to his house and, at the appointed hour, I pulled into the driveway of his home on Mapleton Drive in Bel Air, just south of Sunset Boulevard, and less than a mile from the house on Sunset where I had grown up.

Ray was a guy's guy in every way. He was just plain fun to be around, particularly for me as a contrast to the conservatism of my stepfather. Ray was loose, easy, witty, and very direct. I also had the sense that he was very much cut from the same mold as my father.

Ray was riding very high in 1969. *Funny Girl*, which he conceived and produced, had been the number one box office draw in America in 1968 and had received nine Academy Award nominations.

Ray was amazing that day with me. He told me that he had just been waiting for me to ask him about my Dad.

When Ray met my Dad, back in the 1940s, Ray was an agent at Charlie Feldman's Famous Artists Agency. He and Dad became great friends and Dad helped Ray with his career.

Ray was very aware of my Dad's addiction to painkillers. It was Ray who Mom called when Dad died so that Ray would go to Dad's office at Columbia and make sure no one found any syringes or other drug paraphernalia.

Ray also told me that he had always had qualms about the cover story that Mom had concocted, particularly as it applied to me, so he was relieved to set the record straight.

When it came to the Sinatra story, Ray was a bit reticent about saying too much about the details that Red had told me but he was more forthcoming than my mother had been.

"Steve, your Dad trusted Red completely so he probably knew more details than anyone else."

"Did it happen the way Red said it did?"

"From what I heard, yes, it did. I do know that your Dad made a commitment to Sinatra and Cohn overruled him. Then something happened that made Cohn beg your Dad to come back, that's for sure. Red's story fits all the bits and pieces I heard from your Dad and other people at Columbia."

"Does Mom know?"

"She never discussed it with me and I'm not sure Sylvan would have gone into much detail with her if he even told her at all. Your Mom, bless her, has never been too great with real life, has she?"

No argument there.

"All of that happened so close to Sylvan's death, Steve, that there really wasn't enough time for any of us to reflect on it too much. But, as far as I know, it did happen the way Red explained it to you."

And there it ended. I had heard and learned all I needed to know.

No Place For Old Blue Eyes

Later in 1969, I met the woman whom I would marry in 1970.

We had a whirlwind courtship. She was engaged to another man at the time we met and I had been dating her USC college roommate. We moved in together in the fall of 1969, and, having known each other about four months, were married in January 1970.

As a married young man, things were bound to shift between me and Frank. Life was indeed changing rapidly for me and the moments with Sinatra would become more rare.

It's not that Frank's largesse and kindness ended in 1969. Not at all. It changed, yes, but a moment was about to happen that proved that my godfather was still the same amazing and loving benefactor for me that he had always been.

Frank had not met my new wife. A few weeks after we were married, we were in Palm Springs at Danny Schwartz's house for a party that I had helped to arrange to raise money for John Tunney's senatorial campaign. I had asked Danny to host the party and for Frank to be the guest of honor and they had both graciously consented.

"You bringing that new wife of yours, Stephen?" Frank had asked me on the phone.

"Yes sir, absolutely. She can't wait to meet you," I answered.

We drove down to Palm Springs for the party, which was in full swing when Frank walked in the front door. At that point, people started to applaud, until Frank quite loudly yelled out "I'm not here yet."

(Frank once told me that he had walked into a party and quickly noticed that three of his ex-wives were present. When I asked him what he did, he said, "I decided that was definitely no place for old blue eyes and I left.")

Frank then yelled out "Stephen, where are you?"

We were on the far side of the living room so I somewhat sheepishly raised my hand said "Over here."

Guests parted like the Red Sea as Frank walked directly to us.

When he came up, he went right to my wife and pulled a little jewelry box out of his coat pocket. He then opened it to reveal a small, beautiful diamond on a delicate gold necklace.

Putting it around her neck, he gave her a kiss on both cheeks, and said, "Welcome to the family, sweetheart."

Needless to say, she was utterly charmed.

With that, Frank gave me a big grin and then turned to the party to announce, "Okay, NOW I'm here."

It's important to note that the Palm Springs party happened almost twenty years after my Dad's death, two years after Frank had bailed me out of trouble in Vegas, and almost six years after buying me that great Corvette.

As the years passed, I would still hear from Frank on birthdays and other important events. I saw him at my parent's home a couple of times. I still went to see him perform, sometimes with my folks and sometimes not. He was always kind, loving, supportive, and gracious.

But things had changed.

I was married, albeit briefly.

After two years together, we divorced in 1972.

All In The Family

Frank was also incredibly kind and loving to my sister, Susie, and her children, Don and Janet.

For instance, Susie and her husband Donald were with Frank in Palm Springs at his house in the early 1970s after a social event.

Frank asked Susie why she, as a film critic and writer, had never asked him for an interview. Knowing that Frank hated interviews and wasn't exactly fond of most journalists, she told him that she had never wanted to impose.

Frank asked her if doing an interview with him would be helpful to her career. When she responded with an enthusiastic "Are you kidding?", he asked her if she had a tape recorder with her. She didn't, but Frank found a tape recorder in his house and insisted they sit down right then and there for what turned out to be a two-hour interview that was eventually picked up by the ABC Radio Network.

When the interview was over, Susie thanked him profusely but he just waved her off.

"Susan, you owe me nothing. It's me who should be thanking you."

When Susie asked him what he meant, he got a faraway look in his eyes and simply said "For things that happened a long time ago."

And that was the quintessential Frank Sinatra, as we knew him.

His Way

Frank had taken me under his wing and shown me a great, no, dazzling, time for almost twenty years.

He had more than fulfilled his promise to repay to me the gratitude that he had felt to my father.

Mission accomplished.

Frank faded from my life and we eventually lost touch with each other.

Of course, I kept track from afar of the public Frank Sinatra. His music. His movies. His changing politics. His feuds. His retirement and triumphant comeback.

Through it all, he always had a special place in my heart whenever I saw him on screen or heard his voice on the radio.

When I heard in May 1998 that Frank had died, I was sitting in my home in Tarzana, in the heart of the San Fernando Valley. *What Dreams May Come* was being readied for release that fall so, every day, I was dealing with the film's visions of the afterlife.

I went outside, sat on a lawn chair, and cried.

I had been given the great thrill and honor of knowing and loving one of the greatest and most charismatic entertainers the world has ever known.

I was grateful to have learned so much from him about generosity, loyalty, courage, and style. Oh, did Francis Albert have style.

More than anything, Frank Sinatra taught me how important it was to be my own man, to take chances, and to always be bold in making life decisions. To not fear losing or failure or what anyone thought of me.

In the film *Bandits*, Cate Blanchett has a classic line: "…the heart is a mysterious organ. It plays by its own rules."

In my own heart, I loved movies and knew that my life would always be incomplete if I didn't pursue that dream.

Some people have personalities that are suited to playing it safe in life. For others like me, however, playing it safe is simply a way to avoid failing.

Sinatra taught me that, for better or worse, people do fail at times; however, once you survive that first failure, you know you can survive others. And when you actually realize a dream, the satisfaction is emblazoned more deeply into your soul than any failure possibly could.

Sinatra's lasting legacy to me was to live my life to the fullest, and, of course, to do it "my way."

CHAPTER FIVE

Growing Up in Hollywood: Doesn't Everyone Have a Butler?

"Danger, Will Robinson, danger!"
Lost in Space, 1960s Television Series

My Rise From Abject Privilege

So, what was it like to grow up in a movie business family in Beverly Hills?

I am so acutely aware that my upbringing was so much easier and safer than everyone who grew up with financial and other lifestyle limitations that I cringe when I try to answer the question of what it was like for me.

Obviously, it was one million times easier to grow up the way I did than it is for kids with parents who have to struggle just to put food on the table. To even compare those ways of growing up is absurd in most ways and I know it.

That being said, living inside the bubble of that seemingly idyllic existence was not without its own challenges, even though those challenges paled in comparison to the ones kids faced in the real world.

For instance, I didn't grow up with famous parents but I knew many kids who did. Some of them simply did not have the strength of character to be up to that particular challenge and so they disappeared into drug addiction, overdoses, and even suicide.

Also, many of us became mired in our adolescent emotions and mentalities for many years, if not decades, too long. In fact, I'm not convinced that many of us really "grew up" in the kind of surreal, fantasy life we experienced. We grew older, yes, but many of us, like me, had some real difficulties with the growing up part.

"Mom and Dad Are Rich. You're Broke.

In a few ways anyway, being raised in Beverly Hills in the 1950s was just like being raised anywhere else.

I rode my bike to school every morning, we hung out and played sports after school, and we became the first generation of kids to watch television on a regular basis.

The most popular television shows of the 1950s centered on family life. Problems were always solved by the end of each show and most every character was portrayed as being happy or at least relatively secure.

For me, whatever version of reality that was depicted on shows like *The Adventures of Ozzie and Harriett, Father Knows Best,* and *Make Room for Daddy* was a welcome glimpse into how I thought other families actually lived and was a lot more real than my own life.

Not much else about my early life had any connection to the real world.

Looking back, spoiled and out of touch with reality are descriptions that don't even begin to explain how bizarre it was growing up in Beverly Hills. While I was living it, however, I took almost everything for granted and just assumed that I would always live that kind of life.

In a word, I felt entitled without really understanding what the word meant. I just felt that I would always have money and enjoy the same privileged and easy life that my parents enjoyed.

My stepfather and mother had a full-time chef, two live-in housekeepers, and a butler. Didn't everyone?

I never had to do laundry, clean my room, or do a single household chore. Until I was a teenager, my allowance was whatever I asked for.

Even though "spoiled" is really too polite a word to describe both my lifestyle and my attitude, I was nevertheless convinced that I was untouched by all that extravagance. The only thing I learned about growing up, being responsible, and creating a strong work ethic was…nothing. I was young and my parents were rich, which I foolishly misinterpreted as meaning that I was rich, too.

Oprah Winfrey recently asked actor Will Smith about his kids and their relationship to money. Smith responded with an absolutely classic line that he had said to his son. "Yeah, we had that talk recently. And I said that yes, Mom and Dad are rich….but you're broke!"

Unfortunately, I was blissfully unaware of that simple fact in my own family and was therefore setting myself up to walk the trapeze of life blindfolded and without the net that I had been so certain would always be there to catch me.

Perspective: Isn't That What They Use on Submarines?

One of the first casualties of growing up in a well- to-do Hollywood family is the ability to achieve or maintain any sense of perspective.

Case in point:

One of my stepfather's closest friends and business associates was William (Billy) Goetz. Bill's wife Edie was the daughter of the legendary Louis B. Mayer of MGM (Metro-Goldwyn-Mayer). Along with Joe Schenck and Darryl Zanuck, Billy Goetz was one of the founders of 20th Century Fox and a major film producer (*Sayonara*) in his own right

When I was young, we spent a lot of time in the Goetz's Bel Air home, having elaborate dinners served by a staff of at least four or five people, and then adjourning to their private projection room to watch the newest films from every studio in town.

(My parents also had a private screening room. Actually, it was an entire building behind our house that my mother had my stepfather build so that she didn't always have to go to friends' homes to see movies. Quite appropriately, she named it The Whim House and actually had matchbooks made with that name on the cover.)

Private screening rooms were really the norm for my parents and their friends. Ray Stark had one as well.

Seeing a movie in a theater was much more of an unusual occurrence

In my life than sitting in an overstuffed chair in a private home with homemade popcorn and an endless supply of candy.

I remember wandering the Goetz house one night and noticing that almost every square inch of wall space was covered with art from classic painters. Renoir, Picasso, et al.

I made my way into Bill's study and was immediately struck by the fact that there was only one small painting on the wall.

I thought that was unusual, to say the least. Why only one painting?

My stepfather found me in there and explained that this one painting was very special indeed and that's why it had it's own room.

It was a Vincent Van Gogh self-portrait.

What? Every one didn't visit private houses with Van Goghs and Renoirs, with dinners cooked by personal chefs, followed by first-run movies in a private screening room?

Is There Anyone Here Who Isn't A Movie Star?

My parents entertained constantly and I grew up with a veritable "Who's Who" of Old Hollywood stars and personalities in our houses, first on Sunset Boulevard in Bel Air with my mother and father, then in Beverly Hills with my stepfather:

Frank Sinatra, Mia Farrow, Elizabeth Taylor, Jack Lemmon, Lucille Ball, Cary Grant, Edward G. Robinson, Walter Matthau, Mervyn Leroy, Ronald and Nancy Reagan, Groucho and Harpo Marx, Dean Martin, Sammy Davis, Jr., Kirk Douglas, Gregory Peck, James Stewart, Rosalind Russell, Bud Abbott and Lou Costello, Red Skelton, Judy Holliday, Milton Berle, Danny Kaye, George Burns, Gracie Allen, Jack Benny, Grace Kelly, Henry Fonda, Ruth Gordon, Garson Kanin, Merle Oberon, Bennett Cerf, Laurence Harvey, Truman Capote, Walter and Lee Annenberg, Edgar Bergen (with Charlie McCarthy, Mortimer Snerd, and Candice), June Allyson, Donna Reed, Louis Calhern, Alfred and Betsy Bloomingdale, Ray and Fran Stark, Robert Taylor, Deane and Ann Johnson, Dore Schary, William and Edie Goetz, Joan Caulfield, John Cassavetes, Gena Rowlands, Billy Wilder, Alan and Nancy Livingston, Margaret O'Brien, Lassie (my Dad directed *Son of Lassie*), Johnny Carson, Ricardo Montalban, Gary Merrill, Bette Davis, Tony Martin, Cyd Charisse, Julie London, and, of course, that lovable old Harry Cohn.

Parties and dinners with guests happened at least twice a week in our house, so those names were not just a laundry list.

I remember many of them so well.

I particularly remember the ones who couldn't be bothered with the "boy" of the house and also the ones who made it a point of connecting with me.

Many of the names I listed above are discussed in other chapters so I won't start here. As to some of the others, here are my recollections:

Donna Reed was exactly like the Mom she played on television. She was the real-life Mary from *It's A Wonderful Life*. What a great woman.

Elizabeth Taylor's violet eyes were the most amazing and mesmerizing sight. So much so that it was difficult to actually speak to her. (Many years before, my birth father had owned a horse that he kept at a stables that was very near the MGM lot and Susie rode the horse a lot. One day, Louis B. Mayer, who ran MGM, commandeered the horse for *National Velvet*, in which Elizabeth Taylor starred. My sister always loves to say that "Elizabeth Taylor stole my horse!")

Lucille Ball was a character of epic proportions but she was also simply a warm, friendly neighborhood Mom.

Johnny Carson was a big-time cold fish. It was very difficult for me to connect him with the same guy who hosted *The Tonight Show*.

Gregory Peck also seemed very stiff and unapproachable.

Rosalind Russell, on the other hand, was every inch the character of Auntie Mame. What a hoot she was to be around!

Tony Martin and Cyd Charisse were very down to earth and warm.

John Cassavetes was one of my favorites. He always made a point of spending a few minutes talking to me. It was almost like he knew that film making was in my blood and he wanted to encourage me.

What's the point of listing all these names here?

Simply as a background for how deeply immersed my life was in the Old Hollywood from the day I was born, what a blessing that was, and why it is such an integral a part of my very being that I cannot and will not let it disappear.

The Offspring of Lassie, Cooper, and Benny

As Susie was eight years older than me, some of my first and fondest memories revolved around her and her friends. (Funny, over the years, somehow Susie has evolved into my kid sister. Wonder how that happened, sis?)

Gary Cooper's daughter Maria was Susie's first grade school friend and they have remained best friends to this day.

Elinor Donahue was Susie's other best friend and went on to star in *Father Knows Best*, one of the first huge hit sitcoms.

Susie was also very friendly with Terry Moore (who had appeared in *Son of Lassie*, which Dad directed), Peter Ford (son of Glenn), Joan Benny (daughter of Jack), and Margaret O'Brien.

Birthday parties in The Old Hollywood put the competition between the *Real Housewives of New York City* to shame.

Normal kids had parents dress up as clowns. At Hollywood kid birthdays, that clown would be the real Bozo The Clown, one of the early kids' idols on television.

A normal party at an amusement park would morph into carousels and rides being transported into someone's backyard.

I was not immune either. According to my sister, I desperately wanted a dog. For my third birthday, Dad (who had directed *Son of Lassie*) had Rudd Weatherwax, the trainer of the film Lassies, deliver one of Lassie's offspring to our home.

I also grew up around a lot of kids who had famous parents: Lucille Ball and Desi Arnaz's daughter (Little) Lucie; Frank Sinatra's daughter Tina; Ronald Reagan's daughter Patty and son Michael; Edgar Bergen's daughter Candice; Carl Reiner's son Rob; and Kirk Douglas' son Michael.

Edie Baskin was the daughter of Burt Baskin, one of the founders of 31 Flavors. Edie had an entire 31 Flavors counter in her house, stocked daily in the same the way that all the stores were. Why go to an ice cream parlor when you can just hang out in someone's house?

Dena Kaye was a classmate. Her father, Danny Kaye, was a huge star at the time, both in movies (*The Court Jester*) and on television (*The Danny Kaye Show*). He was also a consummate chef of Chinese food so we enjoyed many of his gourmet dinners in his house. Sure, I knew he was famous but, to me, he was more Dena's father than *the* Danny Kaye.

Two of my stepfather's closest friends were the legendary film director Billy Wilder (*Some Like it Hot, The Apartment, Sunset Boulevard*, etc.), with whom Dad had lunch every week for over thirty years; and also-legendary comedian Jack Benny, who once gave my stepfather a gold money clip with the iconic Benny image etched on it.

A money clip from the "stingiest" man in the world.

"Your money or your life"...."I'm thinking...I'm thinking!!"

Since my stepfather's death in 2006, I have carried that money clip with me every day of my life.

Robby The Robot, Carl Sandburg, Bloomingdale's and Helen Keller

One of my earliest and happiest memories was of a close friend named Nicholas Nayfack, Jr. whose father Nicholas, Sr. produced the iconic sci-fi film *Forbidden Planet*.

Nicky and I spent many a day on the set of the film, getting rides from Robby the Robot, one of the classic and early film robots. For nine-year old boys, that was an all-time rush. (I'm sure we didn't even notice Anne Francis on the set. Years later, when I rediscovered the film, I sure paid a lot more attention to Anne's skimpy costumes than I did to Robby.)

My stepfather's mother, Adele Levy, was a famous New York philanthropist whose closest friends included Eleanor Roosevelt and Helen Keller, the latter of whom I met and spent a day with in Martha's Vineyard, Massachusetts as a young boy. At one point, there was an Adele R. Levy exhibition at the New York Metropolitan Museum of Art.

As a result of my new grandparents, I spent a lot of time in New York and in the late summer of 1960, I spent several weeks with my stepfather as he produced a play that was headed for Broadway.

Entitled *The World of Carl Sandburg*, the play was really a series of stage readings and songs from Sandburg's works. The song troubadour was a wonderful fellow named Clark Allen but the star was none other than Bette Davis.

The play lasted only twenty-nine performances when it hit Broadway in the fall but it was the Los Angeles engagement that set off the fireworks.

Bette Davis' husband Gary Merrill took over the male lead in the play from Leif Erickson and I remember my stepfather saying that he had become more of a referee than a producer.

I also remember meeting the great man himself, Carl Sandburg, in person. Sandburg struck me as one of the kindest, wisest men on the planet.

Speaking of Broadway plays, Betsy Bloomingdale was one of my mother's closest friends. Her husband, Alfred Bloomingdale, told a story at dinner one night that I have never forgotten.

Years before, he had decided to finance a play. While it was playing in Boston, prior to its New York opening, he became nervous about the play's quality, or lack thereof, and invited a theater critic friend of his from New York to come see the play, which the critic agreed to do as a favor.

After a performance of the play, Alfred took the critic out to dinner, waiting to hear some advice, but the critic said nothing at all. Finally feeling frustrated and anxious, Alfred blurted out "Well, what did you think of the play? Can you give my any advice about what to do?"

After reflecting on the question for a moment, the critic leveled a steady eye at Alfred and responded:

"Alfred, close the play…. and keep the store open at night."

Hillcrest: The Last Days of Pompeii

My stepfather and mother were members of the Hillcrest Country Club, a private Jewish club that had been established in West Los Angeles when it became apparent that Jews were not welcome at any of the other golf courses in the area. Yes, anti-Semitism was alive and well even in L.A.

The membership of Hillcrest was a "Who's Who" of the entertainment industry, and Sunday night buffet dinners were the social events of the week.

The amount of food that was displayed on endless buffet tables at those Sunday night bacchanals was famous all over the country.

There was even a very black joke that circulated in the club: "Sunday night buffet dinners at Hillcrest killed more Jews than Hitler."

The other gathering place at Hillcrest was the Men's Grill where a round table in the rear of the room was the unofficial home at lunch time for Jack Benny, George Burns, Milton Berle, George Jessel, Groucho Marx, and others who gathered to share stories and try desperately hard not to laugh at each others' jokes.

I was never allowed to sit at that table but my stepfather did manage from time to time to get us seated at a nearby table so I could overhear snippets of the conversations.

I remember there being a running joke that Berle was going to steal every one's jokes.

I also remember feeling that Groucho's name suited him perfectly. He always seemed so unhappy. I don't think I ever saw him smile.

Elvis Presley, My Sister, and Me

Elvis had appeared on Milton Berle's television show some time in 1957 or 1958.

His manager "Colonel" Tom Parker told Milton that he (Parker) wanted Elvis to experience Hollywood from the perspective of someone who had grown up in that atmosphere. Milton recommended my sister Susie who was about eighteen at the time.

So the date was set up by Milton Berle, my stepfather, and Colonel Parker.

On the appointed evening, Elvis arrived at our house on Bedford Drive in a chauffeured limousine to take Susie to a party.

I was about eleven at the time.

Susie told me that they attended the party and that Elvis was shy, sweet, and a perfect gentleman.

There was no second date.

Fade out.

Fade in a few years later.

Those north/south football games that I mentioned earlier always culminated in a grudge match on Thanksgiving morning in a small park next to a fire station on the corner of North Beverly Drive and Coldwater Canyon.

One day, we were just about to start playing when we noticed three young men saunter into the other end of the park. When they saw us, they walked slowly toward us.

Even from a distance, you could see that there was one normal-sized guy walking in between two other guys who were pretty huge.

When they got close enough, we all immediately realized that the guy in the middle was Elvis Presley.

Elvis came up to us and, in a warm, friendly, and completely humble manner, asked if we had room for three more guys.

Elvis Presley and his two bodyguards wanted to play touch football with us. And they did.

The most remarkable thing about that game was that there really was nothing remarkable about it.

Elvis and his bodyguards simply played touch football with us for a couple of hours. We all laughed and had a great time and there was never a single comment from anyone about our famous playmate for the day.

Obviously, Elvis knew that we knew who he was but, for that day, he just wanted to be a guy playing touch football in a park.

When the game was over, he shook everyone's hand, thanked us profusely, wished us all a Happy Thanksgiving, and left the park as quietly as had entered it.

Other than all that, I led a pretty ordinary *Gump/Zelig* existence. Except for my friendship with the man would soon become President of the United States

CHAPTER SIX

Ronald Reagan
From Horses to the White House

"Being President is all about character."
The American President, 1995

My mother had become friends with Nancy (Davis) Reagan in the 1940s. Nancy married Ronald Reagan in 1952 so the Reagans were family friends from the time I was a very young boy.

Mom, Nancy, Fran Stark, Betsy Bloomingdale, and Lee Annenberg (wife of *TV Guide* founder Walter Annenberg) had all actually become best friends in the 1940s and remained so throughout their lives.

Reagan had been a moderately successful actor then but I started to really become conscious of who he was as the host of television's *GE (General Electric) Theater* throughout the 1950s and into the early 1960s.

Of all my parents' friends, Ray Stark and Ronald Reagan were my favorites.

Reagan was a warm, humble, down to earth guy who always seemed to be smiling and happy.

I had quickly discovered that most of my parents' famous friends had some real difficulty relating to kids like me, but not Reagan. He seemed completely at ease talking with me and, unlike some of the other adults who were always looking around for other friends when they said their perfunctory hellos, I felt that he was genuinely present during those moments.

Horses and Saturday Mornings

Like many boys my age, I had been mesmerized in the 1950s by a serial named *Spin and Marty* that had been a part of *The Mickey Mouse Club*. The series took place on a ranch where kids could ride horses during the summer.

I too loved horses and, in 1960 when I was fourteen, I cajoled my parents into sending me to a ranch/ camp in Mancos, Colorado, near Durango. I loved the camp so much that, for the next three summers, I would leave the day school closed, get on the old Super Chief train, and take it to New Mexico where I would be picked up and taken to the ranch, not to return until the day before school opened in September.

As I was already not getting along with my stepfather, my parents were as happy as I was when I left for the summer.

At the ranch, I owned my own horse (didn't everyone?), a blueberry roan named Shadow. During the summers, she was with me in Colorado.

During the rest of the year, Shadow was stabled at the Reagan's first ranch near Malibu Lake in California.

On many Saturday mornings in 1961 and 1962, I would get a ride out to the Reagan ranch and ride Shadow alongside Reagan on his own horse for at least a couple of hours.

All my parents' friends were addressed as Mr. and Mrs. in those days, but Ronnie, as he was known to his friends, was the first to ask that I call him Ron or Ronnie, not by the more formal Mr. Reagan label. That was so typical of him.

Oddly enough, I had no trouble whatsoever calling Ray Stark by his first name but Mr. Reagan remained Mr. Reagan until he became Governor and later Mr. President.

All the stories about Reagan as a man were, for me, absolutely true. He was simply a terrific guy to hang out with. I did not feel at all close to my stepfather and, at that time, Reagan was temporarily a bit estranged from his own son Michael, so we forged a wonderful bond on those Saturday morning rides.

As we rode together, we talked about a whole variety of things, including his own kids and politics. He had been a Democrat for most of his life but his ideas were changing.

I learned more about current events and government on those Saturday morning rides than I ever did in school.

I soon discovered cars and girls so in 1962, my days at the ranch came to an end, and Shadow stayed in Colorado.

The Gipper Runs for Governor

When I graduated high school in 1964, I attended the University of Pennsylvania in Philadelphia. I desperately wanted to get home to California but couldn't find a way to justify it to my parents until Christmas vacation of my sophomore year.

During that vacation in late 1965, my parents had the Reagans over for dinner. Reagan said that he was going to run for Governor in 1966, and asked if I wanted to work on his campaign.

Reagan was enthusiastic about me working with him and that gave me the perfect way to escape going back to Penn. My parents were not about to argue about me working for their friend as he pursued the governorship and it was Reagan himself who suggested that I transfer to UCLA so I could still attend college and work for him part-time.

Like Reagan himself, my parents had been lifelong Democrats. I too had been drawn into politics by John Kennedy in 1960 and, like most young people at the time, considered myself a Democrat.

I wasn't all that concerned, however, about Reagan's political philosophy at that time because I was mostly focused on Reagan the man. He was someone I deeply admired and respected on a personal level and I was very flattered and excited that he wanted my help, however minor that help might be.

As a result, I dropped out of Penn that Christmas and stayed home to attend UCLA and do whatever I could do to help Reagan become the next governor of California.

Throughout 1966, I took as much time off from UCLA as I possibly could so that I could travel the state with Reagan. I had no official capacity but I was allowed to attend a lot of campaign events and, from time, I woke Reagan up in the morning and was also the last to see him at night.

On election night, I was with the Reagans at election headquarters and was on stage with them when Reagan gave his victory speech. In fact, one photograph from that night that was circulated worldwide featured three people: the Reagans and a very young excited me.

The Governor and Joe Pyne

After the election, the Governor and I talked about me working in his administration.

He felt that I should continue in college and work part-time at something else and I agreed.

With my relationship with the Governor as a calling card, I quickly found a part-time job working for Joe Pyne, who was one the first of the political shock jocks.

In the 1950s and 1960s, Joe blazed the path that personalities like Howard Stern and Rush Limbaugh would follow decades later.

Joe was an acerbic guy whose trademark line was telling callers to "go gargle with razor blades."

When I met him in late 1966, he had both a national and local morning radio show on KLAC in Los Angeles and a weekly television interview show on local station KTTV that was nationally syndicated.

I helped organize callers on the radio and, for television, coordinated the people in the "beef box", where audience members could ask Joe a question.

Joe was a very conservative guy who had lost a leg while serving as a marine in World War Two. He was also very fair-minded in many ways and, even though he was often called a bigot, racism in fact enraged him.

One night, he interviewed than-Governor Lester Maddox of Georgia, whose racist comments so angered Joe that he ended the interview with Maddox by saying "Governor, I've just been informed that there is a freedom bus leaving outside our studio for Georgia right after the show. I suggest you be *under* it."

The Times They Were A-Changing

Even though I still adored Reagan personally and worked for the extremely conservative Joe Pyne, attending UCLA in the 1960s had a huge impact on my own political orientation.

I rather quickly moved farther and farther away from the Reagan political agenda, quit my job with Pyne, and became more politically liberal.

In other words, I was young and it was the late 1960s.

When I saw the Governor and Mrs. Reagan at social functions at my parent's house, it became increasingly more challenging for me to keep my political differences with the Governor to myself.

My mother became so concerned about me offending the Reagans that she stopped inviting me to attend dinners and such when the Reagans were present.

By 1969, my political transformation was complete, and I dropped out of college to again work in politics, but this time it was on the opposite side of the political spectrum.

I became one of the core group of people who worked on John Tunney's first Senatorial campaign in 1970. John was the son of former boxing heavyweight champion Gene Tunney. John's best friend in the world at that time was Ted Kennedy so I was exposed to the Kennedy dynasty that had ignited my political interest in the first place.

In another six degrees of separation oddity, Tunney's opponent was former actor and then-Senator George Murphy with whom my Dad had once made a film and who was also an old acquaintance of the Governor.

By this time, my parents began to see me as a serious liability in their relationship with the Reagans.

Truth be told, the person who was the least fazed by my political reorientation was the Governor himself. He was totally understanding of my political transformation and was actually fond of telling me that I would change again when I got older.

In many ways, he turned out to be absolutely right.

My parents, nevertheless, continued to make me persona non grata at any home events with the Reagans but they needn't have worried so much. Regardless of my political change of heart, I remained enormously fond of Governor Reagan and had great respect for him.

Even though I didn't see the Reagans much over the next ten to fifteen years, the Governor did reach out to me again when he was running for President to see if I had changed my political views. When I demurred, he remained just as warm and friendly.

And I still received warm friendly notes on my birthday from the Reagans, even after the Governor became President.

After he left the Presidency, I did get to see him once at my parents' house and he couldn't possibly have been kinder to me.

Most of my liberal friends in those days had a difficult time reconciling my politics then with my steadfast admiration for Governor and then President Reagan.

To them, I would always say something that I still carry with me in my heart today.

A great guy is a great guy, no matter what you may think of his politics.

And Ronald Reagan was a great guy.

CHAPTER SEVEN

Being the New Kid in Town is Great Fun (Until You Blink and it's Over)

"Please, sir, I want some more."
Oliver, 1968

Calling Ray Stark's Bluff

In my heart, I always knew that I would somehow wind up in the film business but I took a very circuitous route getting there.

Reagan, UCLA and politics in the 1960s, Law School at Loyola in Los Angeles from 1971-1974 and then a very brief stint as a lawyer from 1974-1976 when I operated more as a sports agent than a lawyer. Good thing, too, because I was a pretty lousy lawyer. My clients included such football stars as Ron Jaworski and Jack Youngblood, but my heart was always in a movie theater.

In 1975, I read a book entitled *Bid Time Return* by Richard Matheson, who was one of the deans of American fantasy writing. (Countless *Twilight Zone* episodes, *I Am Legend*, *The Incredible Shrinking Man*, etc.). When I finished the book, I just knew that I had to produce the film version and I began begging Ray Stark to give me a job. (*Bid Time Return* eventually became *Somewhere in Time* and will be discussed in detail in Chapter Nine.)

On a professional level, Ray was the prototype of an Old Hollywood mogul producer. He was a shrewd, creative, and wildly successful film producer and also a brilliant dealmaker.

As a producer, he made a huge string of hits, starting with *Funny Girl*. He also produced *Funny Lady, The Way We Were, The Night of The Iguana, Fat City*, and others. In the 1970s, he began a collaboration with playwright Neil Simon that resulted in such films as *The Goodbye Girl, The Cheap Detective, Murder by Death*, and *California Suite*.

As a dealmaker par excellence, he engineered (through his dear friend Herbert Allen) a complete refinancing and restructuring of Columbia Pictures where he was the string-puller and most powerful single influence.

Ray had a fabulous house in Bel Air where he entertained the crème de la creme of filmdom in his screening room.

On a personal level, Ray had charisma to burn.

He was in his early sixties when I started working for him, but he wore jeans to the office every day and acted more like a thirty year old.

He had a wild, wicked, hilarious sense of humor and laughed heartily much of the time. He played impish practical jokes and squealed with delight when they actually worked.

He had a relentlessly curious mind and was always telling me that he learned something new and exciting every day of his life.

He was neither afraid of nor intimidated by anyone. When it came to taking chances on movies, and cooking up the most brazen and breathtaking schemes imaginable, he had cojones the size of truck tires.

As Ray's wife Fran was one of my mother's the closest friends, Ray was none too thrilled about having to tell my mother that he was going to facilitate my leaving the secure practice of law for the wild uncertainty of a film career.

On the other hand, he had dearly loved my birth father and saw my Dad's passion for movies in me.

I kept after him and, one day in February 1976, in a move he later admitted to me that he thought I would refuse, he offered me a job on three conditions.

First, he would pay me two hundred dollars per week, no more. He knew I was making pretty good money as a sports lawyer and thought I would have to refuse such a pay cut.

Second, I had to start the very next day. Again, he thought there was no way I could leave my practice on such short notice.

Third, I had to agree to sit on the couch in his office and simply observe for three months. No questions, no discussions.

To Ray's shock and chagrin, I accepted all three conditions right on the spot and became his anonymous and voiceless assistant the very next day.

Wedging My Foot and Heart In The Door

True to Ray's challenge, I spent my first three months sitting quietly on the couch in Ray's office, listening to all of his phone conversations, being present at (almost) all of his meetings, and having lunch at least three times a week at Chow's Kosherama, Ray's favorite place for business lunches.

Yes, just as it sounds, Chow's was a Chinese restaurant and Jewish deli rolled into one. Blintzes and egg rolls. Ah, L.A.

Sometimes, Ray would introduce me to people in those meetings. Sometimes, he wouldn't.

None of that mattered to me. I was absolutely riveted to see how a film producer worked.

At that time, David Begelman was the head of Columbia Pictures and was the first person other than Ray to really welcome me into the business. With me, he was a warm, friendly, and engaging man. Later, a huge scandal erupted around a check to actor Cliff Robertson that David had allegedly cashed for himself.

I was actually with Ray in his office in 1977 when Begelman swore to Ray that he had not forged that check. Begelman was lying. He eventually had to resign, and the whole saga became the basis of David McClintock's best selling book, *Indecent Exposure.*

I was ecstatic that I had found way into the first door of the film industry. Yes, my hiring was a direct result of my personal relationship with Ray. Without that, he never would have hired me. But that didn't matter to me. I was in, and I intended to stay in.

Little did I know at the time, but I was about to learn the film business at the feet of one of the last two Old Hollywood master producers.

Years later, I would have the opportunity to work for the other one, Dino De Laurentiis.

I believe that Dino and Ray will always be seen as the last of their Old Hollywood breed.

My magical mystery tour with Ray would last for only two and a half years but what a ride it was.

Neil Simon: The Master at Work

Just before I started to work for Ray, he had begun and then halted production on *The Goodbye Girl*, which Neil Simon had written.

At that time, Neil Simon was the most successful playwright in the world. His string of comedy hits was and still is unparalleled. *Come Blow Your Horn, Barefoot in The Park, The Odd Couple,* and *Plaza Suite* were just a few of the smash hit plays that he wrote.

Neil also wrote the screenplays for the films that were adapted out of his plays and was the only screenwriter that I knew of at the time who had a clause in his contract that prohibited anyone from changing his scripts without his permission. As we will discuss in Chapter Fifteen, that kind of deal is absolutely taboo in The New Hollywood and was pretty rare in The Old Hollywood as well.

Ray had produced the film version of *The Odd Couple* in 1975 and then formed an alliance with Neil that would result in nine more film collaborations.

The most memorable moment for me with Neil was watching him at a script reading of *The Cheap Detective*, an original comedy that he had written and that Ray produced.

Neil and Ray assembled the cast in a private dining room at Trader Vic's Restaurant in the Beverly Hilton Hotel in Beverly Hills.

And quite a cast it was, headed by Peter Falk, Ann-Margret, Madeline Kahn, and several comics like Phil Silvers and Dom de Luise. Cast script readings are fascinating rituals to observe because most of the actors severely underplay their dialogue so as not to have the director and their fellow actors think they are *really* trying.

Undaunted, Neil calmly asked every one to just read through the dialogue. Neil had very kindly invited me to sit next to him.

As the cast read, I saw Neil make notes on his own script. Notes like "works", "OK", and "good" didn't surprise me.

What knocked me out was how tough he was on his own dialogue. He made copious notations that were extremely negative such as ""flat", "bad", and dozens of comments that simply said, "rewrite."

When the reading was over, Neil thanked everyone profusely and told him he would get them all a rewritten script as soon as possible.

As we left the restaurant that night, I asked Neil how he could be so critical of his own work.

His answer has stayed with me until this day, explains why he was so incredibly successful, and is a great message for all screenwriters.

"Stephen, when I listen to a reading like that, I pretend that I have been hired to rewrite the script of a writer I don't like at all. That sure makes changing things a whole lot easier."

From DeNiro To Dreyfuss: *The Goodbye Girl*

Ray and Neil had chosen to Robert DeNiro to play the male lead in *The Goodbye Girl*; however, after a few of weeks of production, Ray shut the film down to recast the lead.

Ray explained to me that DeNiro just wasn't handling the romantic, comedic aspects of the role. (Looking at the DeNiro of today, it's really hard to fathom him not being able to do comedy well. *Analyze This* and *Meet The Fokkers* come immediately to mind. He is obviously now a brilliant comedic and dramatic actor, but thirty years ago, he was still very close to his *Taxi Driver* days and I guess Ray decided that comedy wasn't exactly in his repertoire yet.)

Ray was such a powerful Hollywood player that he could actually decide on his own to shut a film down and start over. Those days are long gone now. Only a studio chief could make that kind of decision today.

Ray and Neil had recast Richard Dreyfuss for the DeNiro role.

As a result of his role in *Jaws*, Richard was riding high in those days. He had also started his career in comedy (*The Apprenticeship of Duddy Kravetz*) so Ray felt very comfortable making the change.

Richard and I had gone to Beverly Hills High School together in 1960-1962 and been friendly, although not close. Rob Reiner, Bonnie Franklin, Candy Marr (later Spelling, wife of Aaron, mother of Tori) and Albert Brooks (then Einstein) were also part of that same class.

Dreyfuss and I had lost track of each other since high school so it was fun for me to see him again in his new incarnation as a big time movie star. Many people over the years had told me that my voice actually sounded like Richard. When I saw him, I asked him if anyone had ever told him that he sounded like me. In his best and inimitable Duddy Kravetz way, he shot back at me: "Of course not. I'm a movie star, Steve, and you're not!" It was said with humor and good spirits and I was really happy for Richard's wonderful success.

The Goodbye Girl went on to become a huge commercial and critical success; moreover, Richard won the 1977 Academy Award for Best Actor for his performance.

While Ray was thrilled by both the success and Richard's triumph, he also voiced a real concern about the effect that the film would have on Richard's career.

Ray told me that Neil had tailored the part perfectly for Richard. Ray was concerned that Richard would then think that he had become a romantic leading man. "As wonderful an actor as Richard is, Steve, he's always going to be more of a character actor. He's at his best when he's playing the every day guy we can relate to like he was in *Jaws*. If he gets it in his head that he's now Cary Grant, he's going to screw himself up."

Ray wanted to have a meeting with Richard so he could give him that advice. I remember arguing vehemently with Ray about the wisdom of having such a meeting but, truthfully, I have forgotten now as to whether or not it ever took place.

The last time I saw Richard was many years later, and now many years ago, when he had just finished shooting *Whose Life Is It Anyway?* He was utterly exhausted and told me that it had been the most draining part he had ever taken on.

Richard went on to make several more memorable films, including *Mr. Holland's Opus*, which is a family favorite and the film that I consider to be his career-crowning achievement. At least, so far.

Jekyll and Hyde and The Blacklist

Ray's company Rastar was run at that time by a producer named Herb Jaffe. When I started working with Ray, he was having second thoughts about Herb and voiced those concerns to me.

I would soon find out that Ray always voiced concerns about anyone who ran his company; consequently, that position was one of the most infamous revolving door executive jobs in the film industry.

Ray's production presidents were faced with what was basically an insoluble conundrum.

If you depended too much on Ray and didn't establish projects and relationships of your own, he would become impatient, decide he didn't respect you for having no initiative, and your shelf life at Rastar would be about two years.

If, however, you charted an independent course, Ray would eventually get jealous, feel left out and insulted, become convinced that you were sabotaging his authority, and your shelf life would still be about two years.

I found a way to learn that lesson very quickly.

At the same time we were working on *The Goodbye Girl*, Ray was also about to go into production on a film called *Casey's Shadow*, which was to star Walter Matthau and be directed by Martin Ritt.

Marty Ritt was an extremely talented, successful, and well-respected director. He had been nominated for an Oscar as Best Director for the classic *Hud* with Paul Newman and had also directed critically acclaimed films like *Sounder*.

On a personal level, Marty had been blacklisted during the McCarthy era and supported himself as a handicapper at the racetrack when he couldn't work on films.

He was a totally honest and decent man of impeccable integrity, so it made little sense to him or most other people including, by the way, Ray himself that he was actually making a movie with Ray.

Ray, however, deeply respected men like Marty so he wanted *Casey's Shadow* to work. Ray also loved the fact that Marty was so revered in the film world and was very proud to be working on a film with him. He quickly made it very clear to me that the Ritt relationship was one he treasured and that he wanted no interference with.

Translation: Stephen, tread softly.

In the film, Matthau played a down and out horse trainer named Lloyd Bourdelle. The plot centered around one particular horse that was treated like a pet by Bourdelle's youngest son.

Marty was intense about the need for reality in the film and Ray was just as intense about his desire for the film to be commercial. (A classic producer/director dilemma.) Ray and Marty had a running conflict about the end of the script. Marty was adamant that he thought the horse needed to die at the end of the film. Ray was horrified and saw that ending as a guarantee of box office disaster.

Marty agreed to shoot the film with alternate endings, one where the horse lived, and one where it died.

Ray was terrified that Marty would insist on using his ending but he also knew that he couldn't overrule a director of Marty's stature. If he did, he ran the risk of not being able to attract class directors like Marty in the future.

That's where I came into the picture, both figuratively and literally.

I was a huge horseracing fan and, as such, had connected with Marty on a personal level.

My passion for horses had started at a very early age because of two wonderful men: Mel Dellar and Mervyn LeRoy.

Mel had been Alfred Hitchcock's first assistant director and also the dean of American line producers. Mel started taking his son Michael and me to the racetrack on a regular basis when we were about eight years old and we were hooked. (Michael and I have been best friends since first grade in 1951 so we're about to mark the sixtieth year of a friendship that I cherish every day of my life.)

Mervyn Leroy was a famous film producer/director (*The Wizard of Oz*) and one of my parents' dearest friends. Mervyn was also the president of the Turf Club at Hollywood Park where I spent many Saturday afternoons.

Anyway, Marty and I hit it off right away when he realized I was a kindred horseracing spirit; moreover, Marty was also a political junkie and we had that in common as well.

Ray couldn't have cared less about either horses or politics. Adding that to the fact that Ray and Marty couldn't have had more different personalities or priorities, they really had no way to relate to each other on a personal basis.

Recognizing that, Ray assigned me the task of politicking Marty about the end of the film. "Do what you have to do to make this work, Steve. The damn horse can't die at the end of the film!"

I already admired and liked Marty enormously, I agreed with Ray about the ending, and spending time with Marty was a total pleasure and fabulous learning experience for me.

Ultimately, Marty himself decided that the horse should not die at the end of the film. Ray was ecstatic and gave me a lot more credit than I deserved for having swayed Marty.

Everything was fine until Ray decided that he wanted to develop another project with Marty.

When we all met to discuss the deal, Marty said he was very interested in the project. He then added: "Ray, if we do this, I just want you to know that I want Stephen here to be the person I work with. He and I worked great together on *Casey's Shadow* and, to be honest, I'm a lot more comfortable with him than I am with you."

Uh-oh.

Marty was just being his typical honest self and I also think that he believed he was giving me a boost with Ray by evincing so much respect for me.

To Marty, Ray responded very graciously but when Marty left, Ray exploded at me and blamed me for everything except maybe the Kennedy assassination.

I had done exactly what Ray had asked me to do but there I was on the brink of being fired.

It was good practice for the five or six times over the next two years that he actually did fire me, only to hire me back the next day.

Except for the last time he fired me. That one stuck.

A quick postscript to *Casey's Shadow*:

Even with the positive ending, preview responses to the film were tepid at best and no one at Columbia seemed to be able to come up with a good marketing hook.

One day, Ray told me that there was a new guy in marketing named Robert Cort who had come up with an idea for a campaign.

When Ray saw Robert's proposed poster for the film, he became so enraged that he actually threw poor Robert up against a wall. I hustled Ray out of the office and shot a quick apologetic look at Robert.

Robert (who had actually worked as an analyst for the CIA before entering the movie business) went on to become a production executive at Fox where in 1983 he oversaw the making of *All The Right Moves* that I produced. He then left Fox to produce hugely successful films (*Three Men and a Baby*, *Cocktail*, etc.) as the head of Interscope, founded by Ted Field, with whom I later worked on both *Bill and Ted's Excellent Adventure* and *What Dreams May Come*.

And that's six degrees of separation in Hollywood.

Smokey and the Bandit: My Vanity Bonfire Ignites

Ray worked the phones from day to night. He was always, and I mean always scheming. He would tell one person something and then immediately contradict himself with someone else.

Bend the truth? Like a boomerang in a typhoon.

I was utterly stunned that he could remember all the contradictory stories he told during the day, but somehow he did. That's one reason that politics and the movie business are so often linked. Show me a good producer and chances are he/she could have been a good politician, and vice-versa.

Ray was also always searching out new ideas, books, scripts, anything that could be turned into a possible film. He would tell me several times a day that the key for me was finding commercial projects and then becoming their champion.

"Be sure you believe in it, pal," he would say "and then never, and I mean, never take no for an answer."

Fortunately for me, that opportunity came very quickly.

Herb Jaffe, who ran Ray's company, was really a fine man but he didn't exactly welcome me with open arms. He knew about Ray's fickle nature and he also knew that Ray was already seeing me as his protégé. To Herb, that meant his job was in jeopardy and he wasn't going to make it easy for me to fit in. He also had every right to resent the fact that a completely inexperienced person like me would suddenly be sitting in on every meeting Ray had. I always understood that and really admired Herb as a man and as a producer.

Ray had another producer under contract named Mort Engelberg. Mort was the exact opposite of Herb. Garrulous, funny, warm, and irreverent, Mort immediately took me under his wing and saw me as more of a potential ally rather than as a threat.

Mort was developing a fun road picture at the time that focused on the hot topic of truck drivers and CB Radios. The project was radically different from the sophisticated movies that Ray usually made and, as such, Mort was having little luck getting Ray interested in making the movie happen.

As I was only thirty at the time, Mort hoped that I would be receptive to becoming an advocate for the film with Ray.

And he was right. I loved the project immediately and saw it as a new kind of film for Ray to champion.

Mort wanted Burt Reynolds to play the lead. Burt had burst on the movie scene just a few years earlier in *Deliverance* in 1972 and then had other hits like *The Longest Yard* in 1974. He had also become quite a celebrity for his famous nude foldout for *Cosmopolitan Magazine* and for his very public love affair with singer/television hostess Dinah Shore, who was several years his senior.

More recently, Burt had made some bad movie choices (*Gator* and *Hustle*) and was looking for a commercial love story/action film.

Burt was interested in Mort's script and wanted Hal Needham, a stunt man friend of Burt's, to be the film's director. Mort had the good sense and sound judgment to wholeheartedly support Burt's desire.

Ray, however, was still not on board.

That's where I came in. Mort asked me to help him sell Ray on the project and I wholeheartedly took on the challenge.

It's important for me to note here that Mort was the force behind the project. He found it, developed it, was the one who got Reynolds and Needham attached, and then went off to produce the film.

My only role was to help convince Ray to get on board and then help find a studio to finance it.

Columbia had already turned it down for basically the same reason that Ray was so indifferent about it. It was considered a redneck movie and nobody other than Mort, and then me, believed in it.

So, I went to work on Ray. Taking his own advice to me, I pestered him mercilessly about it until he finally relented and allowed Mort to set the film up at Universal.

Ray still didn't like the project but he really liked Mort and wanted to support him. He also later explained to me that he saw it as my first chance to prove my worth to him.

As Universal was financing it, Ray got a nice fee out of it and, even if worse came to worse, the film would bomb and he would send me back to my law practice.

If it succeeded, he would know I had some judgment and would reward me accordingly.

In fact, he even had me sign my first contract, which included a tiny piece of the profits from the film. At the time, Ray told me not to get too excited about profits because such an occurrence was highly unlikely.

Mort happily went off to produce the film, now titled *Smokey and The Bandit*.

Mort was and still is an incredibly witty guy. When I asked him what the secret to producing films was, he explained the concept of *per diem* to me. When a producer, actor, or director travels to a location to shoot a film, they get a per diem (per day) allowance for hotels, food, etc.

A thrifty person on location could spend a lot less per day than that per diem. As thrifty was a huge overstatement of Mort's penurious nature, his bottom line advice on the secret to producing: "Get on per diem as soon as you can and stay there as long as you can."

When the film was finished and we saw the first cut, Ray hated it so much that he wanted not only to fire but also to kill both Mort and me. He actually did fire me that first night, only to call me back in the morning and relent.

When he saw the final cut of the film, Ray hated it even more and even called Ned Tanen, the head of Universal to see if he could get his company name removed from the credits.

Oh, and he fired me again. Until the next morning.

Smokey went on to become a gigantic success. It cost about three million dollars and has now grossed over four hundred million dollars.

Ray made over twenty million dollars from the film, making it by far the most personally profitable film with which he had ever been involved.

Despite his animus to the film itself, Ray loved success, was very proud of me, and rewarded me by making me President of his company at the ripe old age of thirty-one.

The New Kid in Town

My first success brought me a new, convertible Jaguar XJS to drive to our offices at Columbia Pictures in Burbank from my new Hollywood Hills home high above the Sunset Strip.

It also brought me a gigantic and insufferable ego.

Agents took my calls right away and I deluded myself into thinking that they actually liked me personally and were my friends.

I dated would-be actresses and again deluded myself into thinking that they were attracted to me personally, which conveniently allowed me to ignore the tiny, little detail that I was the President of a major production company and could help their careers.

To put it succinctly, I was lost in my own ego much of the time, even around my old friends.

I can safely say that the only difference between my own behavior and that of the character Tim Robbins so brilliantly portrayed in the extraordinary movie industry satire *The Player* is that I never actually wanted to kill a writer.

An agent or two maybe, but never a writer.

To this day, I look back on my behavior during those years and shudder but, when I was in the middle of it all, I could explain away or rationalize anything.

My ego knew no boundaries.

In my head, I was a thirty-one-year-old master of the film universe. If there had been a *Bonfire of the Vanities* at that point, I could have provided the lion's share of the fuel.

Even though I had grown up in the film business, I was going to have to learn very soon, and in a very public and painful way, that my egocentric perception of reality and the real truth were separated by a vast ocean of self-delusion.

My career was the Titanic and my ego was the iceberg that was about to gut and sink it.

For the time being, however, I rode the whirlwind and, more often than not, being with Ray was like watching the man behind the curtain in *The Wizard of Oz*.

Ray Seduces Redford, Fonda, and Sidney Pollack

Now that I was the head of the company, I wanted to move quickly and boldly into other projects.

I found a script entitled *The Electric Horseman* that I thought would please Ray enormously because it was just the kind of film he had always loved to make: a compelling love story with two starring roles for major movie stars.

I started bidding on the script only to find that I was competing with Stanley Jaffe, then the production head at Columbia. I told Ray immediately and he called Stanley to say that he wanted to produce the project for Columbia so they shouldn't compete against each other.

Stanley was a very good guy, and a smart one as well. He knew there was no way to fight Ray on something like that. If Ray wanted a project, Stanley knew to get out of the way.

We got the project and Ray was thrilled.

Only then did he even ask me what the script was about.

When I explained the script to him, he got one of those wild gleams in his eye that was always followed by a flurry of "Get me so-and-so on the phone now!"

I was about to see Ray do something that film producers are often accused of doing but few had the guts to even attempt, particularly on the level that Ray was about to play.

If I hadn't actually been there to witness what was about to happen, I wouldn't have believed it was possible.

Two quick notes here.

First, I was aware at the time that Ray had been embroiled in a very unpleasant situation regarding the profits from *The Way We Were*. Evidently, things had become so difficult that Ray wasn't even on speaking terms with either Robert Redford, who had starred in the film, nor Sidney Pollack, who had directed it. (Ray never even talked about Barbra Streisand. Their relationship had imploded several years before.)

Second, as Ray was not a speakerphone, I never heard the other side of the conversations that I'm about to relate here so I can only refer to Ray's running commentary to me about what was said.

"Close the door, be quiet, and watch and learn, Steve. Watch and learn."

His first call was to Jane Fonda who was a huge star at the time and who, fortunately for Ray, had not yet made a film with him and would still take his calls.

"Jane, are you alone?" Ray whispered.

Ray used that opening gambit several times a day. It was his way of enlisting someone into a conspiracy that Ray would make seem like the opportunity of a lifetime.

Ray then proceeded to tell Jane about *The Electric Horseman*.

"The woman in it reads like it was written for you, Jane."

Ray then winked at me as though to say, "Yeah, I know I haven't read it but that has nothing to do with this conversation. Pay attention."

He went on to tell Fonda that Robert Redford really wanted to play the title role, and that Sidney Pollack wanted to direct it, but only if Fonda signed on too.

Excuse me??

As far as I knew, the only thing Redford and Pollack might have been interested in signing at that point was a pledge never to work with Ray again.

Ray leveled a wild, almost orgasmic gaze on me. He was showing off and loving every minute of it.

Ray said he would messenger a copy of the script to her but she had to promise not to say anything to Redford or Pollack.

Evidently, she agreed and Ray hung up the phone. Quickly, he buzzed his assistant Monica to get Redford on the phone.

"Piece of cake, Steve. Piece of cake," he cackled to me in that high-pitched voice he spoke in when he knew he was scamming the system.

Monica buzzed in to say that Redford's assistant said that Redford had no desire to speak to Ray.

Ray quickly picked up the phone and told the assistant that Ray was calling Redford to apologize for all the trouble and to make things right.

Redford then apparently got on the phone.

Ray told Redford how sorry he was for everything and that he had devised a way to make it right. He then told Redford about *The Electric Horseman* and that Jane Fonda wanted to play the part opposite Redford.

I was now absolutely certain that Ray had lost his mind and was about to be exposed by all concerned.

Ray went on to tell Redford that Redford should call Sidney Pollack and get him involved.

"Tell Sidney that I will give him, you, and Jane complete creative control of the film. And you can own the entire back-end (profits). I'll just take my fee and disappear, but you guys have to call off the accountants. I give you this movie and we're even."

Ray hung up and told me "Redford's calling Sidney."

"How do you know he won't call Fonda, too?" I said with my jaw still wide with shock.

"He won't."

"But how do you know?"

"I just know. He won't call her. He's too busy talking to Sidney and, before you ask, the reason I did it this way is that there is no way that Sidney himself would ever take my call."

Sure enough, Redford called back. Ray told me that Redford said that he and Pollack wanted to read the script and that, if they liked it, they would make the deal the way Ray had outlined it.

Redford then said something else and Ray responded. "Yes, tell Sidney I promise never to call him or show up on the set or come to any of the screenings. You guys like this script, it's yours. No strings attached but you have to call off the accountants."

A pause while Redford responded.

"Look, Bob, there's no fraud anywhere. Forget all this if you want and keep after it with the accountants. But, you're never going to find anything wrong and, even if you did, it wouldn't be worth nearly as much as what you and Sidney will make from this new script. Remember, you guys get my producing profits too. So, you in or out?"

Redford said something quickly and Ray hung up.

"They'll do it. I guarantee you they'll all do it. We get a nice fee and the company name on a Redford/Fonda picture and I get those guys off my back. Good day's work. Let's go home."

The Electric Horseman was further developed and eventually shot under the supervision of Andrew Fogelson after I had left the company. (In another example of the revolving and inbred nature of executive Hollywood, and why relationships are so important, Andy was the President of Polygram Pictures many years later when I produced *What Dreams May Come*.)

I was never privy to the final details of *The Electric Horseman* contracts so I don't know how it all worked out, but Redford and Fonda did star in it, Sidney Pollack did direct it, and Andy told me that Ray indeed was forbidden from going to the set.

Hiring and Firing The Most Successful Woman Director In The History of Film: The Skiing Fiasco

Early on in my tenure with Ray, we hired a wonderful young woman named Nancy Meyers to become our story editor.

Nancy was brilliant, utterly fearless, and most impressively, was completely unintimidated by Ray who could be quite a bully, not to mention an unapologetic chauvinist.

Nancy's boyfriend at the time, and later husband and writing partner, was Charles Shyer, who had co-written *Smokey*.

Ray had been developing scripts out of skiing stories forever, but never got one made. As was the ritual for everyone who got my job, and for everyone who got Nancy's job, he insisted that we try to get a skiing script to work.

I committed to myself that I would be the one executive that Ray had ever hired who would actually accomplish the skiing story mission. Little did I know how cursed the whole project was and would continue to be.

We quickly developed a great script called *Freestyle* with a wonderful writer named Ron Koslow who had written the hit film *Lifeguard*.

Unfortunately, Ray had also told Nancy to find a writer and she was also working on the skiing project with a completely different writer.

One company, two writers working on the same project, unbeknownst to each other. Not exactly kosher or honest, and also a violation of several WGA (Writers Guild of America) regulations.

When I realized what was going on, I went to Ray who admitted that he had given Nancy and me the same assignment. (How Nancy and I hadn't even mentioned that to each other will always remain a complete mystery to us both.) I told Ray that we would be in huge trouble if the WGA found out. He told me to shut up, mind my own business, and specifically ordered me not to tell Nancy.

I wish that I could say here that I immediately went to tell Nancy and the writer with whom she was working. But, I didn't. Things were going too well with my career and Ray so I rationalized to myself that I should just shut up and do what my boss had told me to do.

As fate would have it, Nancy ran into Ron Koslow one day in our office and found out what was going on. Immediately, she came to me and said she had to confront Ray. I begged her not to but she insisted.

Sure enough, she quite accurately told Ray that we were way out of line in doing what we were doing and that the writers both needed to be told and one had to cease and desist.

As soon as Nancy left Ray's office, he called me in and told me to fire her immediately and have her get out of the office that day. I argued with him, but to no avail.

Again, I could have refused to do Ray's bidding but I didn't.

I went to Nancy's office and fired her.

In so doing, I abandoned Nancy, failed my own integrity, and betrayed the legacy of my father.

Fortunately for me, Nancy never held what happened against me and she and Chuck remained friends of mine.

In researching this book, I asked Nancy to confirm the details of that sorry moment, and she kindly reminded me that she thought that I felt as bad for firing her as she felt getting fired. She also tried to get me off the hook even now by saying that maybe her writer was working on something other than *Freestyle*.

Whatever the details were, I was complicit in the whole mess, which remains one of my most embarrassing and disgraceful moments.

All I can say now is that I learned a very important and painful lesson that day and was given another chance to redeem myself in a similar situation years later with Ron Bass and Dino De Laurentiis. More on that in Chapter Twelve.

Nancy and Chuck went on to write such huge hits as *Private Benjamin, Baby Boom,* and *Father of The Bride.*

After Nancy and Chuck divorced, she went on to write and direct such smash hits as *The Holiday, What Women Want, Something's Gotta Give,* and *It's Complicated.*

Nancy is now the most successful woman film director in the history of the film business, and deservedly so.

And I fired her.

As I have said before in these pages, a genius I'm not.

Back to the skiing fiasco.

When I read the first draft of *Freestyle,* I was sure that we could make a successful film from it. Ironically, Ray was out of town on one of his skiing trips when I read the script so I decided to surprise my boss.

I called Stanley Jaffe at Columbia and told him about the script. Throughout my time with Ray, Stanley was always really great to me and he was very receptive to reading *Freestyle*.

Before his gig at Columbia, Stanley had already been a hugely successful producer (*Bad News Bears, Goodbye Columbus*) and, when he left Columbia, he continued that success with films such as *Kramer vs. Kramer* and *Fatal Attraction*.

Ironically, he also produced *Taps*, which was the 1981 film that first brought Tom Cruise to my attention for *All The Right Moves*.

Stanley read *Freestyle* immediately and said that he was enthusiastic about moving forward with it.

I was thrilled. I was also certain that Ray would be excited that I had finally justified all the expenses that he had incurred developing ski stories.

I went to Ray's house to meet him when he got home so I could tell him the good news face to face. I was sure that another big bonus would be coming my way.

Ray, however, totally freaked out when I told him that Columbia indeed wanted to make the film.

He was beyond livid (rightfully so) that I had shown Stanley the script before he had even read it. He screamed at me that I was never going to embarrass him again with a movie like *Smokey*. He then told me to go home and pray for my job. If he didn't like the script, he promised to fire me again the next morning and this time he would mean it.

He called the next morning to say that he indeed hated the script and was calling Stanley Jaffe to kill the project altogether. At least, he didn't fire me. He had, however, turned a green light on a film into a red light and I was utterly mystified.

Seeking clarity, I went to see Ray's lawyer, Gerald Lipsky.

I had always been glad to be on Gerry's side. In that way, he reminded me of Jilly Rizzo. If Lipsky was on the opposite side of the table from you, he was one of the toughest guys in the film industry. Behind his desk, he had a huge poster that read:

"Yea, though I walk through the valley of death, I shall fear no evil…for I am the meanest son of a bitch in the valley."

And he was.

When I told Gerry what had happened, he laughed out loud.

"Listen, Steve, this one's my fault. I should have warned you about this. Haven't you wondered why none of the other skiing stories ever got made?"

"Sure," I answered. "They could never get a good script."

"You *are* young," he chuckled. "Look, Ray has been writing off all of his skiing vacations for years against the skiing scripts' development costs. As long as he keeps developing a skiing story, he can take those write-offs. If he actually ever produced a skiing film, there would be no more write-offs."

I was dumbfounded. "You mean he wanted me to fail?"

"Absolutely!" he roared again with laughter. "Welcome to Hollywood, kiddo!"

Ray and I never talked about skiing again.

CHAPTER EIGHT

Never Have Sex With Your Boss's Mistress

"You're not very bright. I like that in a man."
Body Heat, 1981

My Boss, His Mistresses, and Me

On my very first day on the job with Ray in February 1976, he told me that he had a girlfriend whom we'll call Mary.

Ray told me that he had been seeing her for a while and that I was going to have to come to grips with their relationship pretty quickly. He said that I now had to be loyal to him, not to Fran, and not to my mother.

"You're now my assistant. You're on call twenty-four hours a day, seven days a week. Anything you see or hear has to stay between you and me. I need your one hundred percent loyalty and discretion. And no judgments. I'm going to open every door in Hollywood for you. If you have what it takes, you can someday even run Columbia or another studio but you have only one responsibility now and that's to me."

Ray also told me that Mary occasionally spent time at his house when Fran was out of town.

It amazed me that Ray's household staff was so loyal to him that no one ever told Fran anything about what had transpired in her absence.

In fact, Ray employed a cook who had actually worked for my mother before she left to work for Ray. I knew that she was aware of what was going on because, from time to time, she would flash me a little knowing smile when I was in the house with Ray and Mary.

It also made me wonder whether there was some tacit understanding between Ray and Fran but I really doubted that was the case.

One way or the other, Ray had a staff that gave new definition to the word discreet.

Ray also said that he and Mary often met at the apartment that Ray was renting for her, and, from time to time, they traveled together. He also said that we would be occasionally going out together as a threesome so that anyone who saw us would think that Mary was with me; that is, I was about to become Ray's "beard."

He explained to me that he loved Fran deeply, didn't want to hurt her, and would never leave her. He also said that he couldn't completely explain why he had to have someone else in his life besides Fran.

He then added that he had started to see other women six years earlier, right after his son Peter's suicide in 1970. (Unfortunately, Peter wasn't the only person I grew up with who had committed suicide. There were other kids as well who decided that they couldn't live in the long shadows cast by their famous parents.)

I had known Ray and his wife Fran since I was born; moreover, Fran was one of my mother's closest friends. I could have been shocked, distressed, or even disgusted at Ray's infidelity; moreover, I could have refused to be party to it.

I could also tell you that I was deeply offended at Ray's infidelity, that I confronted him with it, and that I demanded that he desist.

Yes, I could say all, or any, of that.

But it wouldn't be true.

I didn't object to Ray's choice in any way at all, and, quite truthfully, I understood, or thought I understood, why Ray had turned to another woman. And it had nothing whatsoever to do with dishonoring Fran, whom I always loved and admired.

Ray had been completely shattered by Peter's death. As tough as Ray was, Peter was his only son and he blamed himself for everything that had gone wrong with their relationship.

I had known Peter fairly well.

Peter was a kind, shy, gentle soul who was temperamentally at opposite poles from his Dad. Ray loved Peter deeply but wanted him to follow a different life path than Peter had wanted to pursue. Ray and Peter had been at loggerheads for years, so much so that Peter had fled to what he hoped would be the cover of the art world in New York so that he could avoid his Dad's long shadow in Los Angeles.

Unfortunately, things didn't get any better.

When Peter committed suicide, Ray took total blame for what had happened. In fact, on the couple of occasions where he actually talked about Peter's death, and there weren't many, Ray told me that he felt that his treatment of Peter "had pushed Peter out the window."

Ray indeed had nightmares about being in the room with Peter when he made the decision to take his own life

In honor of Peter, Ray later established the Peter Stark program for potential film producers and executives at the University of Southern California (USC) Film School.

Rationalizing is More Important than Sex

I thought at the time, and still think, that Ray turned to younger women because he felt that, in some way, he could recapture his own youth and not have to deal with the agony and guilt that the adult Ray experienced every time he looked at Fran or thought about Peter.

Ray adored Fran and I do not believe that he would have taken the chances that he took with other women if he had really been able to cope with his guilt and grief in any other way.

In *The Big Chill,* one of the characters claims that the ability to rationalize is much more important than sex. When challenged on that point, he responds by saying "I can prove it to you. Have you ever gone a week without a rationalization?"

I know that everything I have just written could fairly be interpreted as my own attempt to rationalize both my boss' infidelity to his wife and my acquiescence to it.

I accept that.

Maybe that's true, too. It does not, however, change the feeling that I have in my heart that Ray's infidelity was quite literally the only way he thought he could keep himself alive and relatively sane after Peter's death. That may have been his rationalization, and perhaps my understanding of it is just my own acceptance of his rationalization, but it rang true to me then and the years have done nothing to change my sense of it.

The end result was, of course, that I did not in any way object to Ray's relationship with Mary.

I was also undeniably thrilled at the concept of becoming Ray's main man and was willing to go along with just about anything to be able to learn at the feet of such a successful producer and charismatic mentor.

I had loved and admired Ray my whole life. He was so much fun, so full of life, so irreverent, so bold, so in love with movies, and so completely the opposite of my stepfather, that I wanted to be around him as much as possible.

I also must admit that I wanted to be able to enjoy all the perks that I knew my position would generate.

Ray was the ultimate Hollywood kingmaker. He had installed new management at Columbia and nothing significant happened there without Ray's knowledge.

I was now inside the inside, so to speak. I was ecstatic beyond words, and I sure as hell didn't miss the practice of law, where I had been minimally competent at best. Since the moment I quit law, I have considered myself a "recovering lawyer."

From time to time, Ray indeed did ask me along on dates with Mary as his beard, mostly for film screenings.

Mary was an attractive, vivacious woman so the times we three spent together were, more often than not, easy and fun.

Truth be told, the charade was a pretty flimsy and transparent ruse anyway. Ray's infidelities were not exactly a well-kept secret in Hollywood. Mary, Ray, and I spent several evenings with other friends of Ray at the time and they knew exactly what was going on.

In fact, Ray had gained a rather unpleasant nickname that was only spoken behind his back because it was a name he truly loathed: "Rabbit."

Ray also had a dark side. He could be mercurial, impatient, and judgmental. He also had a fiery temper, and, as I would soon discover, he could be incredibly vindictive.

From time to time, the situation with Mary did ping my conscience, but most of the time, I would just took another whiff of the rationalization opium and convince myself that I was just along for the ride.

For better or for worse, that was me.

I was on the fastest of fast tracks in Hollywood, so I turned a very blind eye to the philandering of my boss.

Until Ray met and started dating the woman who would later become my second wife.

A Long-Tailed Cat in a Room Full of Rocking Chairs

One day in 1977, Ray announced to me that he had broken up with Mary and, before I could ask why, he went on to say that he had met another woman with whom he was completely enamored. He said that he wanted me to come to his house (Fran was out of town) that night to meet her and see a movie.

On my way to Ray's house that fateful night, I remember wondering what had happened with Mary and what this new girl would be like. I was also glad that Ray had also invited *Smokey and The Bandit* producer Mort Engelberg that night. I loved Mort and thought I could hang out with him if the new woman turned out to be less fun than Mary had been.

I walked into Ray's house that night, said hello to Mort, and then was introduced to Jane (not her real name).

Twenty-four, blond, green-eyed, and slender, she was a very attractive young woman. I was shocked that she was actually dating Ray. Huh?

Mary had been world-wise and street-smart. I had never questioned her clear-eyed concept of what she was willing to give to Ray and what she had wanted to receive in return.

Jane, however, seemed completely different than Mary. She had just moved to L.A. to find work as a photographic model and an actress in commercials. To me, she appeared to be an innocent in the lion's den.

What was she doing with Ray, I wondered?

Instantaneously, I felt extremely protective of her and attracted to her, and wildly jealous that she was with Ray.

What the hell was this?

The rest of that night was a complete blur for me. I wanted to ask her what the hell she was doing with a man forty years her senior. I wanted to yell at Ray to leave her the hell alone.

I didn't want to lose my job or offend Ray but this was so different than it had been with Mary. This time, I was engaged as a man, not a willing beard.

More than anything, I wanted desperately to get out of Ray's house just as soon as I possibly could.

When I did finally escape Ray's house that night, it was clear that Jane was planning to spend the night there with Ray, a realization that both sickened and enraged me.

I went home in a befuddled daze. How was I going to even look at Ray the next day?

That night at Ray's house set the tumblers in motion that would completely destroy the life and career that I had built at the time.

The next day, things felt odd with Ray, not from him, but from me.

Whereas I had been more than willing to hear about Ray's escapades with Mary, I didn't even want to hear Ray mention Jane's name. I tried to hide it and would just change subjects when Ray brought up anything about Jane.

My attitude about Ray himself quickly changed as well. Secretly, I became judgmental and disgusted. Behavior I had seen before as youthful and playful became pathetic and even repulsive.

For the first time, I tried to avoid being with Ray on a social basis.

The next time I saw Jane was a couple of weeks later. Ray had insisted that we three go out to dinner together and I had demurred so many times in the interim that I just knew I had to consent.

I met Ray and Jane at Peppone, a tiny, very dark restaurant in Brentwood that Ray loved for dinners with his girl friend and his beard.

The best way I can describe my mood at dinner that night is to say that I was, as an old metaphor goes, "as nervous as a long-tailed cat in a room full of rocking chairs."

As far as I was concerned, we could have been in a *Rocky and Bullwinkle* cartoon. To me, Ray was Snidely Whiplash, Jane was Tess, and I was Dudley Do-Right to the rescue.

Ray was my surrogate father and I was his surrogate son. We both wanted the same woman. No psychodrama going on there, right?

The Hourglass Is Almost Empty

As a result of all the tension around Jane, I started to argue with Ray about business matters as well.

If I had simply sat him down and cleared the air about Jane, maybe things wouldn't have begun to spiral downward as they did.

Ray thought I was being judgmental so he was hurt and angry.

There was another dynamic in the wind with Ray at that time as well.

As I mentioned earlier, running Ray's company meant walking a very narrow and hazardous tightrope. Thanks to *Smokey*, and buying the script of *The Electric Horseman*, the sand in my hourglass was running out.

This was also just about the time when I was trying to make a deal with the Eagles to adapt their extraordinary *Desperado* album into a film.

The Eagles were the top band in the world at that time, I was a hugely enthusiastic fan, and I had become friendly with Irving Azoff, the Eagles' manager and reigning enfant terrible of the rock world in the late 1970s.

I was always very fond of Irving even though he was, without question, the most aggravating tennis player ever on the planet. He returned everything, never tried a passing shot of his own, and just waited for his opponent to miss, which I always did. As a consequence, I don't remember winning even a set from him, an occurrence that pleased him immensely and irritated the hell out me. In fact, if he reads this, I'm sure he'll be grinning like a Cheshire cat.

Unfortunately, the dramatic rights to *Desperado* were hopelessly entangled with two New York stage producers named Steve Lieber and Jim Krebs.

After losing a few more tennis matches to Irving at his Benedict Canyon home, I made him a proposal that he accepted: If I could somehow manage to disentangle the rights situation, and if Don Henley and Glenn Frey met and approved of me, Irving, Glenn, and Don would then agree to make a deal with us on *Desperado*.

I was just cocky enough to think I could make that happen.

I met Glenn and Don and explained my vision of the film to them. They were very anxious to get the dramatic rights back, Irving had endorsed me, and I know they were amused when I told them my fantasy about "New Kid in Town" being written about me. I accepted their unconvincing explanation that, since they had never met me, I was mistaken. Even though my ego saw that as a flimsy excuse, I gracefully decided not to argue with them.

They agreed to move forward. There was, however, one caveat. They had heard some disturbing tales about Ray and they wanted to be assured that they would not be getting the rights back from people who had not consulted with them, just to cede them to someone else who would run off and do the same thing.

I explained all that to Ray, and told him that I had to give my word to Glenn, Don, and Irving that we would consult them, in a meaningful way, at every step along the film pathway. Even though he was a bit irked that they would ask, and that I had agreed to ask him, he agreed.

We got everybody together in an office in Los Angeles and managed to make the deal.

At the time, I thought I had just manifested a miracle and, of course, handed the success directly to my ego. Now I was sure that I was a genius and that my ascension to studio head would happen in a matter of months, not years.

(I also wanted to try to make a film out of Stevie Nicks' classic song, "Rhiannon." Irving set up a meeting for me but I am embarrassed to say that I was so flummoxed by actually being in a room with Stevie Nicks that I stumbled and bumbled like a complete fool.)

We were in the midst of the *Desperado* process while Ray was dating Jane.

One day, Jane came to the office to see Ray, and she stepped into my office to ask if we could meet for lunch that coming weekend.

She told me that she really needed advice, that she couldn't ask Ray, and that she really wanted to speak to me. She also said that she didn't want Ray to know and that I shouldn't meet her if I felt I would have to tell Ray that we were getting together.

She seemed very open in that moment with me, confusing me even more. I told her that I would have to think about it and she left.

What to do?

Could, should, I go meet Ray's mistress and not tell him?

I went through an internal charade in which I "thought long and hard about it", but the truth was that I had decided to meet her the minute she had invited me.

There was no logic to it. I knew I shouldn't do it. I just knew that I was going to do it.

That next Saturday, we met for lunch at a restaurant in Westwood called The Old World.

Jane told me that she felt extremely uncomfortable with Ray, that she had jumped in way over her head, that she wasn't attracted to him, but that she was also very grateful that he was introducing her to a lot of people who could help her career and that he was paying for her apartment. She didn't know how to handle breaking up with him and wanted my advice.

I jumped in and told her that I was relieved to hear her say all those things because I had been having such a hard time seeing her with Ray.

I also added that I really shouldn't be talking to her and that I needed to go.

Which I did. I abruptly stood up and left the restaurant.

I drove home that day, telling myself that this was nuts, that I was out of mind, and that I should stay as far away from her as humanly possible. But I was fighting a losing battle with myself.

That night, I had sex with my boss's mistress.

Sex, Lies, and Betrayal

I often wondered later what might have happened if I had confessed my feelings for Jane to Ray, and simply begged forgiveness.

This was, however, a sex and rationalization concoction, chased with a healthy shot of Shakespearean father-drama, self-destruction, competition, and poor self-image, so I chose to ignore all of it and just focus on the fact that she now wanted me and not Ray.

All that was left was telling Ray.

When I finally mustered the courage, we sat down in his office.

I stammered and stuttered all over the place as I explained to him what had happened between Jane and myself; that I had fallen in love with her and she with me; that was she was moving in with me; and that we had already started to discuss getting married.

Ray exploded like an erupting volcano.

"Are you out of your goddamn mind? You lied to me? You did this behind my back? I can't believe you would have been so fucking stupid!" he bellowed at me.

I tried to stay calm and even attempted to apologize but I was also furious at his attitude about her and we just went at each other.

Ray was hurt and angry that I would betray him and he was even more incredulous that I would risk everything for Jane.

"Has she got you so whipped now that you really don't see who this girl is?" he yelled. "Her agent sent her in to meet me and she was all over me from the minute she walked in the door."

"Oh bullshit," I yelled back. "You're just pissed that she's with me now."

Ray was as red in the face as I had ever seen him.

"This girl seduced me, not the other way around. Before I knew it, I was paying for her apartment. She knows what she wants and she knows how to get it."

By time, I was reeling and Ray could tell.

"Stephen, you should see some of the notes this girl has written to me. There's something wrong with her, I swear to you. Wake up!

I'm pissed at you, yeah, but I'm also not going to let you throw your life and career away on this girl."

I was completely stunned and sat there in silence.

He went in for the kill.

"Stephen, I swear to you that this will ruin your life. Not just your future with me and your career but your entire goddamn life."

As much as I wanted to yell back at him, I was so completely taken aback by his vehemence that I didn't know what to say or do.

He was angry with me, yes, but it seemed that he was also trying to be protective of me. That really confused me. Was he just trying to sabotage Jane and me or was he really overcoming his own sense of betrayal and looking after my best interests? Was this my boss whom I had just betrayed or a protective father figure or both?

"You want to throw your life away on this girl, Stephen?" Ray repeated. "Do you really want to do that?"

"I'm so confused now, Ray. I don't know what to say."

"Then get out of here for the day. I'll get a ride home from someone around here. Go home and think about what you're about to do."

With my head spinning, I managed to drive home, but I was more confused than I had ever remembered being.

Jane came over, reassured me that everything would work out, and moved in with me that night.

The Self-Destruction Cocktail: Arrogance plus Ego

When I saw Ray the next day, he was very subdued. He didn't apologize for anything that he had said, but he wasn't breathing fire any more either. He simply said that we needed to move on and that my personal life was my personal life and he would accept that.

On the surface, then, I hoped that maybe I had weathered the crisis and things could go back to the way they were, but that was not to be. It was foolishly naïve of me to have thought we could overcome what had just happened.

Ray decided that he would drive himself to work every day.

We met only to talk about company business and then only when necessary.

He never asked about Jane, and we never socialized.

Quite simply, what had been was no more. The personal relationship between Ray and me had been torn asunder.

It never even occurred to me that my career was in any kind of real danger. In my ego's distorted image, I was much more than the flavor of the month in Hollywood. I was, I thought, the next Louis B. Mayer.

Smokey was a huge success, I had become the Eagles' savior, and I had just bought *The Electric Horseman*.

As far as I was concerned, there hadn't been a young executive with my kind of talent and vision since the legendary Irving Thalberg. I was sure that every studio in town would offer me carte blanche if Ray dared cross me.

We had made the *Desperado* deal with the Eagles. I reminded Ray about the promise I had made to Glenn Frey, Don Henley, and Irving Azoff about them having meaningful consultation about the screen-writer, etc. Ray heard me but he wasn't listening.

Just before Jane and I got married, I found out that Ray had hired Frank Pierson to write the screenplay for *Desperado*. Even though Frank was a terrific screenwriter (*Dog Day Afternoon, Cat Ballou*), The Eagles weren't even informed, let alone consulted, and neither was I; moreover, with all due respect to Frank's prodigious skills as a writer, he didn't seem to be the right guy to adapt a rock album.

I asked Ray what had happened. He told me that it was none of my business and that he would oversee the project himself from then on.

I knew that he was throwing down the gauntlet in front of me but I also knew that I had given my word to The Eagles. I told Ray that I was duty-bound to inform The Eagles about what was going on, and reminded Ray that he had authorized me to make that promise on behalf of our company.

He ordered me to say nothing and I told him that I couldn't do that.

Sure, it was his company but how dare he think that I should listen to him about how it should be run?

I called Irving Azoff to inform him about what was going on and also told him that I was about to get married and would get back with him once we returned from our honeymoon.

The Dark Side of The Moon

At that time, my lawyer was Tom Pollock, who later became the President of Universal. When we returned from our honeymoon, Tom, who was also a close friend, called to tell me that Ray had tried to fire me for telling The Eagles about *Desperado* and for other unspecified reasons.

Tom had then pointed out to Gerry Lipsky, Ray's lawyer, that Ray had no legal grounds to fire me, and so if Ray did indeed fire me, I would still be entitled to the small percentage of the profits from *Smokey* that had Ray had given me. When Tom demanded that they make a settlement if they wanted me to leave, both Ray and Gerry went ballistic.

I was about to live through my own psychological version of what Richard Gere's character endured in *An Officer and a Gentleman* when the Lou Gossett character did everything he could possibly imagine to get Gere to drop out of the training school.

Ray took away my office and my assistant and relocated me to a file room.

I was informed that my job was now to reread every script Ray had ever developed and submit feasibility reports on the suitability of those projects as television movies.

In other words, Ray was trying to get me to quit, rather than fire me and have to make some kind of settlement with me on the profit percentage he had promised me.

I had stepped directly into the crosshairs of the darkest side of Ray and the vindictiveness for which he was so feared but which I had never personally experienced before.

From the moment Ray fired me, almost none of those agents whom I thought were my friends would even take my calls. They were already out partying with the next new kid in town.

There's a poignant moment in the film *Wall Street* where the character played by Charlie Sheen is about to be arrested for securities fraud. His boss, played by Hal Holbrook, puts his arm around Sheen's shoulder and says, "A man looks into the abyss and sees nothing looking back at him. That's when you find your character and that's what keeps you out of the abyss."

Unfortunately, my own character was so weak and unformed at that time that there was absolutely nothing to keep me out of the abyss. So, I plummeted headlong into it and crashed with a resounding thud.

Welcome to the real Hollywood, Stephen.

On one level, I know Ray was upset that I would turn my back on becoming the executive that he had been grooming me to be. Although I blamed him at the time for being jealous, impossible, and just plain mean, I now see that he was, more than anything, deeply hurt that I would get into a conflict with him over a woman. In that regard, he was indeed acting like the father I had always wanted him to be, but I couldn't and wouldn't recognize it.

There's a scene in *What Dreams May Come* that also mirrors where I was at that moment.

Max von Sydow tells Robin Williams that he can actually take Robin to find his deceased wife in her own afterlife experience. He warns Robin, however, that, no matter what, she won't recognize him, so fierce is her denial of reality. That denial, Max says, is stronger than her love; in fact it is reinforced by her love.

That's where I was with Ray. He was angry, yes, but, more than anything, he was trying to protect me and I was in just too much ego denial to recognize or acknowledge it.

On an even deeper level, Ray felt betrayed by his surrogate son, reopening the wounds from Peter's death.

Looking back now, Ray was completely right.

My actions were those of a spoiled, arrogant, self-righteous, and self-indulgent child. My ego had become so artificially inflated that I thought I was immune to anyone and to anything. I was also taking out on Ray all the rage I had felt but never vented at my father for dying and thus abandoning me

I was on the brink of a meteoric career but, underneath, I had powerful feelings of fear and inadequacy that made me feel unworthy of any kind of real success or happiness. I saw the opportunity to snatch defeat from the jaws of victory and welcomed it with open arms and a healthy dose of self-loathing.

I spent an utterly demoralizing month during my exile to the file room. Tom wisely counseled me to keep my head down and do what they demanded of me for a while. He told me to be pleasant and polite if I ever saw Ray in the hallway outside our offices.

Tom felt that Ray would eventually cool down and that, even if he didn't, the pressures from the family relationships at play would ultimately cause Ray to relent.

Eventually, a settlement was indeed reached, and I was greatly relieved that the whole mess was over.

Or so I thought.

Ray was about to blackball me at every studio in Hollywood.

Blackballed

Yes, we had reached a settlement of my contract, but Ray was still angry. As a consequence, he then tried to blackball me throughout the business by telling other studios that he would not work with them if they did business with me.

I had contacts with junior executives at some of the major studios at that time and a couple of them confirmed to me that Ray had indeed delivered such an ultimatum to their bosses.

Ray was as powerful a producer as there was anywhere at that time and nobody was willing to cross him for some kid who had merely enjoyed a couple of successes under Ray's tutelage.

Only Ned Tanen, then the head of Universal, would allow me to even develop a project there as a producer. That project turned out to be *Somewhere in Time,* the only Rastar project that I had been allowed to keep in my settlement.

One More Chance?

It took almost three more years for Ray and I to speak again, but in 1981 he called me to his office.

By then, I had produced *Somewhere in Time,* had other projects in development, and really wanted to make peace with and maybe even ally again with my old boss and mentor.

I had even convinced myself that we could even produce some movies together. I had betrayed him, he had blackballed me, and so to me we were even.

I dearly hoped that we could shake hands and start over. And I had missed him.

When I walked into Ray's office, I felt such a sense of sadness and melancholy that tears immediately filled my eyes.

It was the same office in which I had spent so many wonderful and electric moments. The office where Ray had hired me. The office where I had learned the film business.

Ray's assistants had changed in the previous three years. They didn't know me, and I didn't know them, but I had the sense that they knew of me.

Years later, I was reminded of that moment when I saw *The Hours*. There's a scene in the film near the end in which a mother, played by Julianne Moore, arrives immediately after the suicide of her son, whom she had abandoned as a child. When she enters the apartment, the character played by Clare Danes looks at her and says, "So, that's the monster."

That's how I felt when I walked into Ray's office that day.

Ray didn't get up from behind his desk to greet me, and my heart immediately sank. So much for my visions of rapprochement.

He just said a very detached "Hello" and motioned for me to sit down. We both then kind of stared out the window in a moment of supreme awkwardness.

Two strangers in a very strange land.

The exact details of what we said now elude me. I know that we both said the right things. "Sorry." "Me, too." "How are you?" "Fine."

We went through the motions, yes, but everything that we had shared, everything that we had been with and to each other, was gone forever. There had just been too much pain and drama to bridge the chasm between us.

After a few brief moments, Ray got up and stuck his hand across the desk to say good luck and good-bye. We shook hands briefly, avoided each other's eyes, and I was out the door, walking to my car, feeling empty, sad, and guilty.

For all that had been. For all that was never again to be.

I think Ray was acting that day more out of respect for my mother than anything else. I had known him well enough to see that his heart just wasn't there that day.

I knew that Ray felt that I had betrayed and abandoned him and that I had also blown my potential career as a studio executive over the situation with Jane. And, he was right.

I was guilty on both counts.

I very well may have had a chance to *become* a studio head one day if I hadn't crossed Ray. I was on that track and Ray was the ultimate kingmaker. I'm also not sure that I would ever have *succeeded* doing that kind of job even if I had attained it.

I was never suited for it and I truly think that I might have failed pretty miserably even if I had ever been given such a chance.

Maybe I'm doing some *Big Chill* rationalizing again, but I just did not possess the skill set that it took then, and still takes today, to be the head of a studio.

A studio executive needs to be more of a judge, and I have always been much more comfortable as an advocate, which is the role of a producer and/or director.

I also never cared much about the politics of the business, nor did I embrace the constant socializing that led to the relationships that led to the green lights on films.

On my best day, I was never more than a B player in the film industry and, truth be told, I spent most of my career in the gentleman's C category. In any case, I loved and still love the making of movies and I am beyond grateful for every opportunity I ever had.

Bankruptcy, Divorce, and Despair

In November 1988, Jane suffered an emotional breakdown and things went from worse to horrendous.

The trauma of the next couple of years led not only to a painful and contentious divorce, but also to bankruptcy for me as well.

We had been living way beyond our means and my financial status depended on me making a movie almost every year. The proceeds from that new movie would then pay the taxes and debts due from the year before, and so on.

In essence, I was living inside a Ponzi scheme of my own making.

Sometimes, life becomes so askew and so littered with the debris of bad decisions that it cannot be fixed. Like an old car that can no longer be repaired and must be replaced altogether, life sometimes forces us to accept that our lives are beyond repair.

And that's exactly what happened to me in 1990.

My marriage ended, my house went into foreclosure, my car was repossessed right out of my garage, I declared bankruptcy, and I almost lost custody of my children.

In the depths of despair over losing everything, I discovered that I could never really lose everything. I only lost the symbols of the parts of my life that no longer worked.

When I hit bottom, and began to climb out, I knew I could survive anything, and failure never seemed as frightening again.

The Way He Was

Even though we had formally reconciled in 1981, that awkward meeting in Ray's office was the last time I saw or spoke to Ray for more than twenty years.

I could have, should have, contacted Ray after Fran's death in 1992, but I didn't.

I had not heard from him after my divorce in 1990 and I assumed, and rationalized, that he just didn't want to be in contact with me. I knew that he had heard about what had happened from my parents but he had not initiated any contact. He would have been completely justified if he had wanted to engage in a major "I-told-you-so" conversation, but it never happened.

He wanted no part of me, and I completely understood.

It hurt, but the damage had been done and I also knew that I had been the one who had caused the rupture in our relationship.

Sadly, Ray suffered a debilitating stroke in 2002.

I had already moved to Oregon but I did visit L.A. occasionally and, on one of those trips, I went to see Ray as he recovered.

I had called his secretary to ask if I could come to see him and waited for a reply. I had no idea if he would even be willing to see me, so it came as a great relief when his secretary called me back and told me that he would be happy for me to visit.

There was a surreal moment as I pulled into the driveway of the Mapleton Drive house where I had spent so much time. The tension eased for me and I smiled when I saw the police car from *Smokey and The Bandit* that we had placed in Ray's driveway to scare away unwanted visitors. After more than twenty years, it was still there, standing guard.

I was ushered into the one of Ray's living rooms, directly off the garden that was dotted with Henry Moore statuary. Ray's screening room was only about ten feet away.

I had to take a breath to steady myself when I saw Ray, who was sitting in a chair with a nurse sitting next to him.

I had heard that Ray's stroke had been quite severe but I still wasn't prepared for the man in that chair.

Certainly, Ray had aged. That I had expected. He had been sixty-six when I had last seen him but he had been a very young sixty-six. The eighty-six year old man I saw that day was a mere shell of the Ray I had remembered, loved, and betrayed.

He was old, ill, and very, very frail.

He was dozing when I came in. When I sat down in front of him, his nurse gently squeezed his hand and called his name. His eyes fluttered open and he looked right at me. His eyes were glassy and his mouth drooped. The stroke had indeed taken a terrible toll.

The nurse urged me to remind Ray who I was so, haltingly, I did just that.

It was then that I saw a glimmer of recognition. His eyes focused even more and I knew that he recognized me. Even though the lump in my throat felt like a grapefruit, it felt wonderful to be with him again, even under those circumstances.

Even though his words were spoken very softly and somewhat garbled, Ray could speak. His nurse also served as a sort of translator.

Ray told me that he was glad to see me but that he didn't recognize me with my beard. I had grown the beard in 1980 and he had in fact seen me with the beard at our last meeting in 1981, but it was understandable that he remembered me clean-shaven, which I had been throughout my years with him.

He then mumbled something else that was translated to me by his nurse.

"How's Sylvan?" he had asked.

It had been fifty years since my father's death but Ray was asking about my father in the present tense. Whatever state of mind he was in at that time, he spoke of my Dad as though he was still alive. To Ray, maybe he was.

After that single question, his eyes closed again and his nurse indicated that the visit was over. I got up quietly and left.

As I drove away, I was lost in a daze.

I had intended to drive farther down Mapleton and around the small park off Beverly Glen Blvd. just south of Sunset so that I could get a firsthand look at the monster mansion that Aaron Spelling and his wife (and my former schoolmate) Candy had built.

Seeing Ray made me just want to drive to the beach and so I did, passing my old house on Sunset as I drove.

The vibrant, larger-than-life kingmaker that I had loved, emulated, feared, resented, and respected was no more. It broke my heart to see him that way. He was such a proud man that I could only imagine how frustrating it was for him to have to fight his way back from such a devastating blow.

Bye, Pal

I went back to see Ray again several months later and was thrilled to see that he was much, much improved.

He was walking again, albeit slowly and carefully. He knew me immediately and we talked briefly about old times. He even made a quip about a mutual acquaintance that let me know his wit was still there.

After a few minutes, I knew it was time to leave.

Ray was sitting in his chair.

Quietly, I got up, leaned over, and gently patted his hand.

"Bye, Ray."

He looked up and smiled.

"Bye, pal."

He hadn't called me "pal" in over twenty years.

Words cannot express how grateful I was, for in that one moment, I was back in the good times with the man I had loved so much. The man who had made my career and life possible.

I promised to come back and see him next time I came to town, but that next time was not to be.

Ray died at the age of eighty-eight in January 2004, several months after I saw him for that last time.

Without Ray Stark, I never would have had a film career.

Under Ray's tutelage, I had a meteoric rise as a young executive, delivered that success on a platter to my ego, and then had to learn in a painful and public way that I was a legend only in my own mind.

I destroyed my career in a heartbeat because I lost sight of what had propelled me into a movie career in the first place.

I wanted to tell stories that would move people's hearts and inspire them to be the best version of themselves. Of course, I overlooked the tiny, insignificant detail that I needed to be that kind of person myself before I could even think of inspiring anyone else

Ray Stark had been my Dad's friend and protégé, my mentor, my surrogate father, my mother's dear friend, my teacher, my inspiration, my idol, my boss, my nemesis, and my rival.

If anyone wants to make a film (or German opera) out of all that, the rights are available with only one proviso:

I'd like Hugh Jackman to play me.

And so would my wife.

My father, S. Sylvan Simon

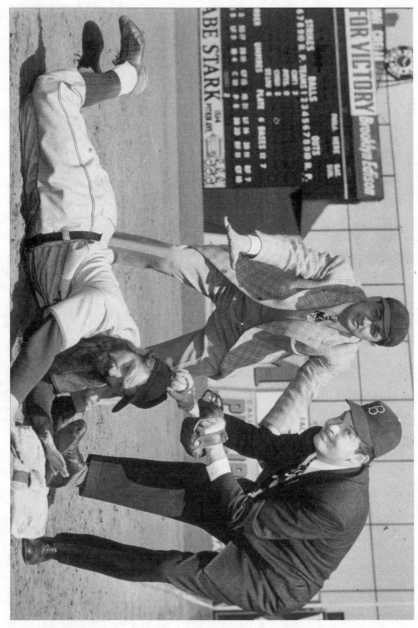

Red Skelton (sliding) Milton Berle (ball and glove) and Dad

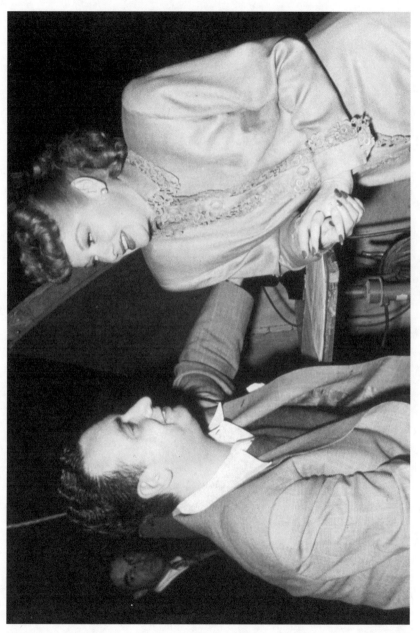

Dad and Lucille Ball

Dad, Bud Abbott, and Lou Costello

My sister Susan, Wallace Beery, and Dad

Lana Turner, unidentified man, and Dad

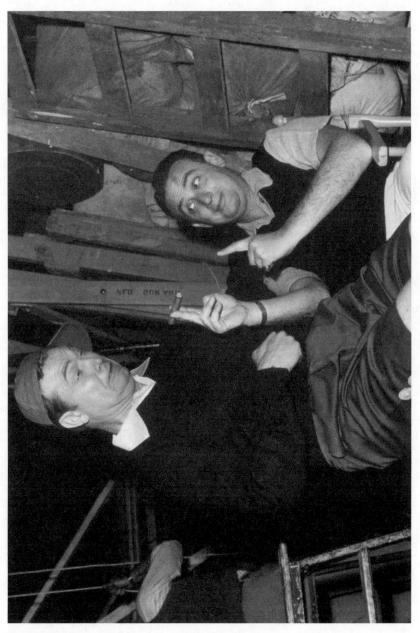

Red Skelton and Dad

My sister Susan and Lassie

My mother Harriet Deutsch and Frank Sinatra

(L to R) My stepfather Armand Deutsch, Lee Annenberg,
Frank Sinatra, my mother, Walter Annenberg

Frank Sinatra and my stepfather

Ambassador Walter Annenberg's Party Celebrating Lee & Harriet's
50th anniversary of our friendship — Bistro Garden — Aug. 1988

My mother, President Reagan, Lee Annenberg (1988)

Courtesy: The Ronald Reagan Library

Dear Harriet—
@ fun evening— love
Nancy
1982

Nancy Reagan and my mother (1982)
Courtesy: The Ronald Reagan Library

(L to R) My stepfather, Kirk Douglas, Fran Stark, Anne Douglas, Ray Stark, my mother

(L to R) Claudette Colbert, my stepfather, my mother, Rosalind Russell (1961)

Jack and Mary Benny

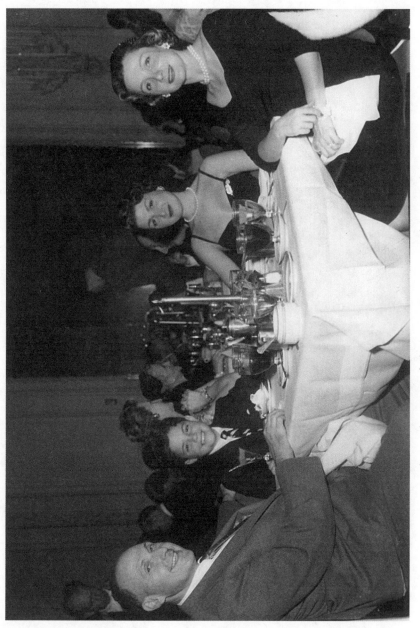

(L to R) My stepfather, me, my sister, and my mother

(L to R) Me, Orvil Dryfoos (President, later publisher of *The New York Times*), my mother, Marian Sulzberger Dryfoos, my stepfather. Opening day of Disneyland, July 18, 1955.

Me and my sister!

CHAPTER NINE

Somewhere in Time: A Box Office Disaster Becomes a Cult Favorite

"Is it you?"
Somewhere in Time (1980)

Amidst the mistakes and ego trips of my career, there were also moments of grace and wonder.

Immediately after Ray Stark hired me, I sought out Richard Matheson, who had written *Bid Time Return,* the novel that had propelled me to beg Ray for a job.

I contacted Rick Ray who was the agent representing Richard at the time. Using Ray Stark's name was a no-limit credit card with almost everyone in Hollywood and a lunch with Matheson was quickly arranged.

I adored Richard from the minute I met him, he agreed to option the novel to us, and a lifelong friendship began.

Even though Ray had allowed me to option the rights to the project from Richard Matheson right after he hired me in 1976, Ray never had even the slightest interest in the project.

I realized that all I could do for the time being was bide my time on *Bid Time Return.* (Sorry. Couldn't resist.)

Fortunately, fate stepped in to push the project along.

Universal had, of course, been thrilled with the results of *Smokey and the Bandit* and Ned Tanen, the production head at the time, was extremely gracious to me.

One day, Ned mentioned a director named Jeannot Szwarc who had come in during production to replace the director of *Jaws 2*. Universal was very happy with Jeannot and the film.

When I mentioned the conversation to Ray, he immediately suggested that I set up a meeting with Jeannot to see if we could all find a project to do together.

"Way ahead of you, boss. He's coming in tomorrow," I was happy to respond.

The next day, we met with Jeannot, who turned out to be an outgoing, utterly charming guy.

When Ray asked Jeannot what kind of film he would like to do next, Jeannot got a wistful look on his face and said "What I would really love to be able to make is an old-fashioned romantic love story like *Portrait of Jennie* in the 1940s."

"Boy, do I have a book for you!" I yelled out while Ray's eyes rolled back into his head. This was not the direction he had wanted the meeting to take.

The die, however, was cast.

Jeannot read and loved *Bid Time Return*. Ray didn't want to develop the script at Columbia so we made the deal with Universal.

We were still developing the script when Ray fired me and agreed finally to settle my contract. The only project that I was allowed to take with me was the film adaptation of *Bid Time Return*, which had not yet been titled *Somewhere in Time*.

All my producing eggs were, so to speak, in that one basket.

Ray, however, was hell-bent to smash all the eggs and burn the basket.

You Better Not Work With Stephen, Or Else

Producers always try to have as many projects in development at the same time as possible, thus increasing the chances that at least one of them will get produced.

I had one project and one studio that would work with me. For a film producer, those odds were not exactly cause for unbridled enthusiasm.

Ned Tanen, the head of production at Universal, was, however, a stand-up guy.

I was actually in Ned's office one day when his assistant came in to say that Ray was on the phone. Ned motioned for me to be quiet and put the call on speakerphone.

Ray started out with that phrase I had heard him utter thousands of timed before. "Are you alone?"

He then told Ned that he would never again make a movie at Universal if Ned worked with me.

Ned paused a moment, winked at me, and then said quite simply "Do you promise, Ray?" and hung up the phone.

Universal owed a big debt of gratitude to Jeannot Szwarc, the director of *Somewhere in Time*, because he had done a terrific job when he replaced the original director of *Jaws 2*. They liked Jeannot a lot and really felt they owed him something. Regardless of what came next, Universal never would have made the film if Jeannot had not been the director.

Ned also knew that I had championed *Smokey*.

I will also always believe that Ned was so offended by Ray's Machiavellian attitude towards me that he continued to develop the film as much to support Jeannot and spite Ray as he did from belief in the film itself.

Oh, and there was the small detail of casting the hottest actor in the world to play the lead. More on that in a moment.

I've had the good fortune to have had some wonderful helping hands in my career. None bigger or timelier than those of Ned Tanen.

Sadly, Ned died recently at the age of seventy-seven. He was a great, great guy.

Get Christopher Reeve or Don't Come Back

It was by now late 1978.

Universal was fine about developing the script for *Bid Time Return* but getting them to green light the film was an entirely different matter.

Our film was an old-fashioned fantasy love story in a year in which two of the three highest grossing films were *Grease* and *Animal House*.

Superman, the other highest-grossing film of 1978 wasn't even released until December of that year and starred a hitherto unknown young actor named Christopher Reeve who immediately became the hottest young actor in the world.

Every film project has a moment in which it reaches critical mass.

For us, in early 1979, we were at that moment.

Universal was either going to green light it or abandon it. And it all would depend on whom we would cast as the lead.

A meeting was called in Ned's office for Jeannot, myself, and our production executive, Verna Fields.

As a producer, it is absolutely essential to have an ally on the studio executive team. Executives have frequent meetings where decisions are made about the films that are going to be made and those that are going to be abandoned. If a producer has an ally in those meetings, that executive can argue the case for the producer and the film. Without such an ally, there is no one to plead your case.

Analogizing this to a courtroom setting, the head of production is the judge and the executives are the attorneys who offer various arguments. A producer without an ally in those meetings would be like a defense attorney who is barred from the courtroom while only the prosecution team is allowed to argue to the judge.

Our executive Verna had been a legendary film editor, editing such films as *American Graffiti, What's Up Doc?*, and *Jaws*, for which she won the Academy Award as Best Editor. An incredibly loving and supportive person, Verna became affectionately known as "mother cutter".

Universal had enormous respect for Verna and she was the only executive at Universal who supported our film.

Before we entered what we knew was going to be a fateful meeting with Ned, we three discussed possibilities for the lead.

Completely offhandedly, I mentioned Christopher Reeve as a possibility even though I thought at the time that it was a ridiculous notion. Reeve was being offered every movie for which he could possibly be considered and was fielding financial offers that were half of our entire budget. Verna wanted Reeve to be put on the casting list but we all agreed that we should be careful about not creating an expectation that we could get him. We didn't want to be in a position where Ned would just focus on a long shot like Reeve.

Into the meeting we marched.

I knew we were in deep, deep trouble when Ned started off by saying "You know, I love you guys…"

Uh-oh.

I knew the biggest "but" in the world was about to escape Ned's lips so I just blurted out "What if we get Christopher Reeve?"

Immediately, I tried to backtrack but to no avail.

I had given Ned the perfect no-lose scenario for him and the studio. Get Reeve for his first film since *Superman* and Universal had a coup. Don't get Reeve and at least Ned would have given us a chance at our green light.

I tried every other dodge I could think of but the die was cast. When I tried to reason with Ned by pointing out that Reeve was himself getting offers of two million dollars, Ned just smiled.

"Seeing as you guys only have four million dollars to make the movie, you better get him for a lot less than two million dollars."

"So, we're supposed to get the hottest star in the business for a salary way below his price, for a movie you don't want to make and no one else at Universal other than Verna even understands?"

"Good, Stephen," Ned laughed. "Now you're catching on. You may have a future as a producer yet....if you get Reeve."

With that, the meeting was over and we left the Ned's office.

Even A Blind Squirrel Finds An Acorn Every Once in a While

When we reconvened in Verna's office, we determined that the most we could afford to pay Reeve was five hundred thousand dollars, about twenty-five per cent of what he was getting offered.

Jeannot looked at me like Oliver Hardy used to look at Stan Laurel.

"Another fine mess you've gotten us into."

And he was so right.

I dreaded the call I was about to make to Chris' agent. When I mentioned the five hundred thousand dollar offer, the agent just laughed at me and told me to forget about it.

I didn't blame him. I wish I could have forgotten about it too but we were where we were.

We could not go back to Ned.

We couldn't get Chris' agent to send him the script.

We decided that we needed to find Chris on our own but we didn't know how.

There was one alternative that was so bizarre that I didn't have the nerve to mention it to Jeannot.

Alone, I went to Sunset Boulevard, bought a map to the stars' homes, and hoped that somehow Chris would be listed.

A quick note about star maps. They were and still are sold to people who want to see the homes where the stars lived. Being a Southern

California native, I knew how unreliable many of the addresses were.

After all, someone can tell you a star lives in a certain house but, unless that person happens to be out front mowing the lawn, how are you going to know who really lives there?

Still, I thought it was worth a shot and, sure enough, there was a listed address for Chris Reeve.

Without telling Jeannot how I found the address, and without knowing if it was reliable, Jeannot and I took a script with us and off we went.

When we got to the house, we walked up and rang the doorbell.

And Christopher Reeve answered the door.

When we managed to close our gaping mouths, we quickly explained who we were and why we were there.

When I got to the point of telling Chris that his agent had refused to even send him the script, he got a very strange look in his eye and invited us in.

For a few minutes, we explained the project and also told him up right up front that we only had five hundred thousand dollars to pay him. He seemed completely unfazed by the salary issue and very intrigued about the love story.

He promised to read the script that night and asked us to come back the next day.

When we arrived the next morning, Chris told us that he loved the script and he committed right then to star in the film for the salary we had discussed the day before. No negotiation.

We had our star.

Years later, Chris told me that we had also benefited from the timing of our visit. He had just read a script that his agent had sent him in which he was being asked to play a Viking. Not a football player. The marauders of the past. Those Vikings.

When he envisioned himself in one of those inverted gourd Viking helmets, he was horrified, and then in walked this gentle love story.

A Warning from Michael Douglas

I was flush with confidence (arrogance?) again.

The new kid was back.

We had Christopher Reeve for his first film since *Superman* and I was on my way to being able to produce all the movies I had ever dreamed of.

Or not.

One day as we prepped the film, I ran into Michael Douglas. Even though our parents were good friends, Michael was a couple of years older than me and while we were cordial when we saw each other, we had never been friends.

I very proudly told Michael that I was about to produce my first film. With a knowing smile, he asked me to sit down for a few minutes so he could tell me something important about producing movies.

Michael's first film as a producer had been *One Flew Over The Cuckoo's Nest*, which received multiple Oscar nominations.

Michael told me that, just before he attended the Oscar ceremony, he set up meetings for the next day with several studios so that he could try to make a deal on the next film he wanted to produce.

He told me that he was confident that *Cuckoo's Nest* would win at least one or two Oscars and he wanted to strike while the iron was hot, so to speak.

One Flew Over The Cuckoo's Nest actually won five Oscars that night, including the one that Michael personally won as the producer for Best Picture. In fact, *Cuckoo's Nest* became the first film in over forty years to sweep all the major categories: Actor, Actress, Director, Screenplay, and Picture.

The next day, flush with that success, Michael went to his meetings, certain that he would be besieged with offers to produce the film that he was pitching.

He was rejected by every studio.

Every one.

The day after winning the Oscar for Best Picture.

(The project he had been pitching was The *China Syndrome* and it actually took him almost four years to get it made.)

"So look, Stephen, I didn't tell you this to scare you. It's just a really important thing to know. Actors, directors, they can live off hits for a while. As producers, we start over from scratch every time."

He had told me the story with great humanity and very warmly wished me the best of luck with my film as he walked away.

Michael had given me a wise, compassionate piece of advice and, of course, I managed to ignore it almost immediately.

Summer of Love At The Grand Hotel

To find Chris' love interest, we had meetings with almost every young actress in Hollywood, until Jane Seymour walked in the door in character, and in a period dress. She stayed in character the entire time. Both her reading with Chris and her chemistry with him were off the charts and we offered her the part that day.

We knew that *Bid Time Return* was not a great title for the film. One day, I heard an old Barry Manilow song entitled "Somewhere In The Night" and the title *Somewhere in Time* was born.

The big puzzle piece that we did not yet have was the location.

The script called for an old hotel that had been around since at least 1912. As we had severe budget restrictions, we needed to be able to shoot the 1912 sequences in a location that was untouched by modern day devices like parking meters, etc. The book had been set at the Hotel del Coronado near San Diego but the area was too modern for us.

And then we heard of The Grand Hotel on Mackinac Island, Michigan.

The Grand had been built in 1887 and the photos we saw were beyond magnificent. We were also thrilled to hear that motorized vehicles had never been allowed on the Island and that taxis were actually horse-drawn carriages so there were no modern impediments of any kind.

The challenge, of course, was that we would need our equipment trucks. Other than a brief sequence in a 1946 film, no one had shot a film on the Island because of those logistical challenges.

I discovered that the Grand was actually owned not by some big corporation but by one man, Dan Musser. I sent him a copy of the script, noting that his hotel would be one of the major stars of the film.

Mr. Musser called very soon after he read the script and invited us to come visit the Island, which we quickly did. We fell in love with the hotel and the island, leading Mr. Musser to say that he would make things work for us.

And did he ever.

Mr. Musser and his entire staff facilitated the shooting at his always busy hotel and he even forged a way for us to get permits for a couple of trucks on the Island.

On the end credits of the film, we thanked Mr. Musser and his staff for "the gracious use of their magnificent hotel."

Without Dan Musser, *Somewhere in Time* would have been a very different and lesser film.

The On and Off Screen Love Story

If you've seen *Somewhere in Time* and felt that the chemistry between Jane and Chris was intense, you couldn't be more correct.

The hottest rumor of our truly idyllic shoot was that Chris and Jane were carrying on a torrid love affair.

Another thing they managed to keep as a secret from me (and our insurance company that would have gone ballistic if they knew) was that Chris kept a small private plane hidden on the island. Every weekend, he and Jane would fly away.

Superman carried Lois Lane off in his arms but Chris needed that plane.

The Film Crashes and Burns

Somewhere in Time was released in October 1980 and completely bombed, both with critics and at the box office. The reviews were particularly harsh about Chris. I'll never forget Chris' anguished call to me when he read one particular review that cruelly described him as something of an overstuffed canary in his period costume.

If you put your heart and soul into a film because you really believe in it and it fails, the pain is very real. You have to be a pretty callous and cynical person not to feel the sting of a box office and critical failure such as we experienced with *Somewhere in Time*.

In other words, it hurt. It hurt like hell.

While we were all devastated by the film's flameout, I felt that I had particularly and personally let Richard Matheson, Jeannot, Chris, and Jane down.

We felt that we had made a beautiful love story but, suddenly, it was gone.

HBO and The Z Channel: A Cult Film Is Born

For the first several years of its existence, HBO had a very limited nine-hour broadcast day. In late 1981, however, HBO started to broadcast twenty-fours a day. Consequently, its appetite for films grew voraciously and one of the films it licensed in those early days was *Somewhere in Time*.

At the same time, The Z Channel had launched in Los Angeles as one of the first pay cable stations in the United States.

Z was programmed by a film aficionado named Jerry Harvey who also just happened to be one of the few people who had seen *Somewhere in Time* in a theater in 1980.

Jerry contacted me at that time to tell me how much he loved the film and that he was going to program it for Z, which he did.

In those early days of Z, there were only two film showings per evening. Not only was *Somewhere in Time* shown constantly on Z, there were a few evenings when Jerry programmed it as the only film of the night.

After having quickly disappeared in 1980, people started to discover *Somewhere in Time* in the mid-1980s.

A Smash Hit. In One Theater

In 1984, *Somewhere in Time* opened in one theater, The Palace, in Hong Kong, China.

The film then played there continuously for eighteen months, ultimately becoming one of the top ten grossing American films in the history of Hong Kong.

Along with the devoted following that the film was building through its cable screenings, a cult film was in the making.

INSITE:
The International Network of *Somewhere in Time* Enthusiasts

In 1990, a wonderful man named Bill Shepard championed *Somewhere in Time* with such passion that he decided to start both a fan club and a newsletter devoted exclusively to the film. Without Bill Shepard, *Somewhere in Time* would have probably faded away.

The newsletter that Bill launched has been continuously published on a quarterly basis since 1990 and is still going strong, as is the fan club for the film.

A lovely and dedicated woman named Jo Addie, who was an extra in the film itself, has now taken over for Bill and has also created a huge line of *Somewhere in Time* collectibles. (www.somewhereintime.tv)

The Annual *Somewhere in Time* Weekend

Since 1991, INSITE has sponsored a yearly *Somewhere in Time* weekend at The Grand Hotel in Michigan where the film was shot.

The hotel is always sold out for the weekend of activities that include screenings, a trivia contest, scene reenactments during a guided tour of the island, and a 1912 costume ball on Saturday night. Film professor and author Steve Ellis does a great job of coordinating the weekend.

People come from all over the world and bring elaborate period clothes in which they often dress for the whole weekend. I first attended one of the weekends in 2000 and went again in 2003. In 2009 and 2010, Lauren and I brought most of the family with us and had a fabulous, magical time.

On This Spot in 1912

In 1993, INSITE, with the permission of both Mackinac Island and the State of Michigan, placed a permanent plaque on the exact site where Chris and Jane's characters first meet in the film.

The plaque reads:

"Is it You?

At This Site on June 27, 1912

Richard Collier Found Elise McKenna."

When I saw that plaque for the first time in October 2000, I realized that *Somewhere in Time* had truly found its audience.

Costner's Law

Kevin Costner once reportedly said that the real test of a film is time. If, a few years after a film has been released, someone has it in their DVD collection and lends it to a friend with the recommendation of "You have to see this", then the film is a success.

Although I have never had the thrill of producing or directing a film that was an unqualified box office success, I do now know the satisfaction to which Kevin Costner so perceptively referred.

A film that stands the test of time and builds a passionate audience provides a particularly deep sense of pride and gratitude.

So, to all of you who brought *Somewhere In Time* out of the shadows, please accept the most profound appreciation of all of us who worked on the film.

Tragedy Strikes

Chris and I stayed in sporadic touch over the years, including a couple of discussions about the possibility of him directing a film that I would produce, but nothing ever materialized.

Then the news came of his horrific accident in 1995.

It seemed incomprehensible that Chris Reeve, whose whole life had been highlighted by physicality, would be so traumatically injured.

Coach Pete Carroll Throws a Hail Mary

Less than twenty-four hours after Chris' accident, I received a phone call from Pete Carroll, who at that time was an assistant coach with the New York Jets.

Coach Carroll had somewhat miraculously tracked me down through my involvement with *Somewhere in Time.*

Pete explained to me that Dennis Byrd, a football player that he had coached, had suffered the same kind of injury that Chris had suffered but had received a very specific treatment right after the injury that made it possible for him to eventually walk again.

I had never met Chris' wife Dana so I had no real chance to be able to talk to her. I did, however, know Gae Exton, whom I had met during the *Somewhere in Time* shoot.

Gae had been Chris' girlfriend back in the late 1970s and 1980s and, even though they had never married, Gae is the mother of Chris' two kids Matthew and Alexandra.

I found the name of the hospital where Chris was being treated, called the emergency room, and convinced a nurse there to hand Gae a message to please call me because I had some information that could be crucial for Chris' recovery.

Within an hour, Gae called me back and I explained everything to her that Pete had explained to me. She listened very intently, told me that she would absolutely tell Dana right away, and promised to call me back when she had more to tell me.

True to her word, Gae did call me back a couple of days later to say that the potential procedure had indeed been discussed with Dana and the doctors but that the decision had been made not to pursue it.

I have every faith that Dana and Chris's doctors made the right decision, as I obviously have absolutely no idea that the procedure would have helped Chris even if it had been tried.

After I heard from Gae, I called Pete Carroll back and thanked him profusely for his efforts. He had gone way out of his way to try to help someone whom he had never met. I really admired that and him.

In fact, his compassion was so sincere that I became a lifelong Pete Carroll fan that very day.

Pete went on to become the head football coach at The University of Southern California (USC) where he won two national championships. While Pete was at USC, I even shifted my allegiance from my alma mater UCLA to our archrival USC.

In the spring of 2010, Pete left USC to become the head coach of the pro football Seattle Seahawks. For me, that was a double stroke of good fortune. I can root for my alma mater again and also for a neighbor here in the Pacific Northwest.

In researching this book, I contacted the Seahawks office and relayed a message about what I was doing to Pete's wonderful assistant Dawn.

True to form, Pete graciously took some time from his hectic schedule to return my call so that I could refresh my memory about our conversations of fifteen years ago.

Pete Carroll is a class act.

Somewhere in Time Premieres—Twenty Years Late

Somewhere in Time became such a video hit in the 1990s that Universal financed a new documentary in 2000 about the making of the film and A Collector's Edition Video/DVD was planned for October of that year.

To launch that new initiative, Universal actually planned a theatrical premiere showing of *Somewhere in Time* for October.

The film originally opened in October 1980 during a strike by the Screen Actor's Guild so neither Chris nor Jane had been able to do promotion for the film or attend a premiere that we actually never had.

On October 24, 2000, the premiere happened and I saw Chris in person for the first time since his accident five years before.

He was in wonderful, even ebullient, spirits that night and I was just thunderstruck at his strength, courage, and character. He was much more concerned about everyone around him being comfortable than he was with his own situation.

Chris' sensitivity to those around him was also highlighted that night when he insisted that his chair be wheeled out to the front of the theater in darkness before the lights went up to introduce him. He didn't want people to feel uncomfortable seeing all the wires and attachments on the back of the chair.

Having not seen Chris in many years before that night, I was awestruck by how much he had grown as a man. I know that may sound odd but it was so clear that Chris had become much more than an actor who had suffered a disastrous injury.

He had become the living symbol of a cause. Not just for people with catastrophic spinal injuries, but for all those people like him who had decided to become stronger and more luminous souls after their injuries.

I felt so very proud that night that I knew Christopher Reeve, the human being, not the actor.

Christopher Reeve and *Illusion*

In 1997, Chris directed an HBO film titled *In The Gloaming*, for which he was nominated for an Emmy.

I had always wanted to make a film version of Richard Bach's classic novel *Illusion*. In 2002, I suggested to Richard Bach that Chris would be a great director for the film and Bach enthusiastically agreed.

I contacted Chris, he read and loved the book, and we had several phone conversations about the book and other matters. (He was kind enough to read and then give me a wonderful endorsement for the back cover of my first book, *The Force is With You*.)

In those conversations, I noted how alive his sense of humor had become. He just loved laughing about himself. He also told me that he had received some advanced treatments and that he had actually some movement back in one or two of his fingers. For someone with the kind of spinal cord injury that Chris had suffered, this development was something akin to miraculous.

I then traveled to Chris' home in Bedford, New York to discuss putting the film together.

When I arrived, Chris couldn't wait to tell me what had happened when his friend Treat Williams had come to visit. When Williams walked in the room, he saw Chris and said "Hey, Chris, good to see you. Don't get up."

Chris had such a twinkle in his eye when he related that story. He just loved that his friend had been comfortable enough to joke with him.

He also proudly showed me how he could move one or two of his fingers.

A few minutes later, he showed me again. Then again.

He then asked if I wanted to see his fingers move again and I told him no, that I had seen enough and it wasn't all that thrilling after the first time.

"Oh, who cares what you want?" Chris smiled. "I'm going to show you as many times as I damn well please."

And so it went for almost an hour.

His assistant had told me in advance that the meeting would last no more than thirty minutes so as not to exhaust Chris, but Chris was excited about the possibility of directing the film.

He also told me over and over that he was going to get out of that chair eventually. He absolutely believed it and I absolutely believed him.

Near the end of our meeting, Chris said that he wanted to ask me a very serious question.

"Go ahead," I replied.

"Steve, do you really think I can do a good job of directing this or are you just doing this as a publicity stunt?"

Without hesitating, I responded, "I saw your HBO film. You couldn't even direct traffic, pal, but we'll hire good actors and the publicity will be incredible."

His face lit up like a pinball machine as he exclaimed "The truth. The truth. A producer finally tells the truth!"

It wasn't the truth at all, as I explained when the moment passed. He had done a terrific job on the HBO film and I thought his accident had made him so acutely sensitive to the human condition that he would do a terrific job directing the film.

We said goodbye for the moment and I told him that I would be back after I made the deal with Bach and obtained financing for the film.

For various reasons, neither happened.

The Real Superman

When I heard of Chris' death in 2004, I was stunned.

I had been certain that he was not only going to live on but that he was going to get up out of that chair and walk again. The man who played Superman became the real Superman for the world after his accident.

Chris' energy, courage, and dedication to making lives better for all victims of spinal cord injuries will live on forever.

Two years after Chris' death, his wife Dana died of lung cancer, even though she had never smoked and was only forty-five years old.

The similarity to the end of *Somewhere in Time* is strikingly poignant.

A loved one dying of a broken heart to join her soul mate in eternity.

I'm sure Chris was there, reaching out with his hand and his heart to welcome her home.

CHAPTER TEN

Tom Cruise Makes
All The Right Moves

*"The football team at my high school, they were tough. After
they sacked the quarterback, they went after his family."*
Back To School, 1986

In 1981, I made a producing deal with Twentieth Century Fox and
moved onto the Fox lot in West Los Angeles.

The prime architect of my deal there was distribution head Norman
Levy who had previously been at Columbia when I was with Ray Stark.
Norman and I had always worked well together and it was he who
forged the way for me at Fox.

In addition, Sherry Lansing was then the head of production at Fox
and was the first woman ever to achieve that title. Sherry had been a
friend of mine at Columbia as well.

Fox was owned at that time by Marvin Davis, a somewhat
enigmatic but wildly wealthy oil tycoon. One of Marvin's closest friends
in Hollywood was Gary Morton whom I also knew fairly well because
he was married to longtime family friend Lucille Ball. Gary had also
been an actor (*Lenny*) and comedian and had always wanted to get into
film production.

Norman and Marvin asked me to share offices with Gary and help
him get some movie credits. I had always liked Gary and so the deal
was made.

What Happens If The Good Guys Lose?

Early on in my deal there, I read an article by Pat Jordan in *Sports Illustrated* about kids in struggling Pennsylvania steel towns. The only way for them to get out of that environment was to win football scholarships so the parents groomed their children for a football career as much as possible.

Some families even went so far as to hold their kids back in elementary school for a couple of years so they could be bigger and stronger when they entered high school.

I thought it would be a good idea to develop a sports film based in one of those steel towns and that we should try to do something different in a sports film: have the big game occur in the middle of the film, rather than at the end, and have the good guys lose. The rest of the film would then look at the consequences of that loss for those kids.

Mass-market commerciality has obviously never been one of my strengths but I didn't want to just repeat the conventions of every other football film ever made.

Fox liked the idea so we hired a writer named Michael Kane to write the script. I had known Michael from the Rastar days when he wrote a script for us called *Hot Stuff*. Michael was also a huge football fan.

The script was wonderful and we hired Michael Chapman as the director. Michael was at that time one of the premier cinematographers in the world. He had just been nominated for an Oscar for his work on *Raging Bull* and had also shot other films like *Taxi Driver*. A mutual friend named Phil Goldfarb had told me that Michael really wanted to direct a film.

Michael turned out to be a truly brilliant, no-nonsense New Englander who seemed to be (and was) the perfect choice for the sensibilities of *All The Right Moves*.

Casting Tom Cruise

Michael and I had both seen Tom in a small role in a film called *Taps* and were absolutely convinced he was the right guy to star in our film.

Tom's agent at that time was Paula Wagner (who later became his producing partner). She set up a meeting for Michael and me with Tom.

One of the things that Michael and I had decided about the cast was that every one had to at least look like they could still be in high school. Tom had just turned twenty but he had a very boyish look.

He also had what can only be described as "it."

There is something about certain young actors and actresses that sets them apart from most of the peers: presence, charisma, an aura of inevitability, confidence, charm, and a sense of "beingness" that radiates an unmistakable essence of talent.

I had seen "it" before when we cast Jane Seymour in *Somewhere in Time* and I would see it again in later years in Charlie Sheen, Matthew Perry, and others.

With Tom, it was just unmistakable. Star quality emanated from him like a beacon in the night.

Tom had committed to starring in *Risky Business* but had not yet started the film. Paula knew that Tom was getting very hot at that time so she asked us to pay him one hundred and twenty-five thousand dollars to star in our film.

Tom has now received about two hundred times that salary for films, but, back then, he was still an unknown and Paula's salary demand temporarily scared Fox away.

Enter my old friend Robert Cort, the ex-CIA agent whom Ray had thrown up against a wall at Columbia over the ad campaign for *Casey's Shadow*.

Robert had just become a production executive at Fox but another executive named Dan Rissner had been assigned to our film. I went to Sherry Lansing and begged for Robert to replace Dan as our production executive. Sherry was a little dubious about the change but she ultimately relented and Robert took over.

Robert completely agreed with our assessment of Tom, successfully argued our cause with the other executives, and Tom got his "massive" one hundred and twenty-five thousand dollar payday.

Please Keep Your Clothes On!

We did some casting in Los Angeles but Michael had a strong feeling that the rest of our young cast, particularly the young men who would have to be believable as steel town football players, would be better found in New York. We also needed to find our female lead, the young girl with whom Tom's character would fall in love.

Michael and I then spent the better part of a week in casting sessions with Pat McCorkle, our New York casting agent. Spending that week in New York was memorable for me for several reasons, not the least of which was the fact that Michael Chapman had been the camera operator on *The Godfather*. Six degrees of separation again.

Every night, Michael led me to one of those impossible-to-find family restaurants in Little Italy with authentic Italian cooking. I was in foodie heaven.

We read dozens of young women for the lead in the film but were most impressed with a young actress named Lea Thompson, who had not yet acted in a feature film.

We told Pat that we wanted Lea and a couple of other young women to read with Tom, who graciously came to New York to participate.

Lea was by far and away the best actress in the reading and there was great chemistry between her and Tom.

After the reading, Tom departed, and we told Pat that we wanted to offer the part to Lea.

"You guys sure she is the one?" Pat asked Michael and me.

"Absolutely," we answered.

"Good. I'll make her the offer subject to her coming in here and taking her clothes off in the office with the three of us."

The script called for a very explicit love scene between Tom and Lea's characters. Early on, Pat had asked Michael if nudity was going to be required and Michael had said yes. It was, after all, a love scene and a critical point in the film. It was never going to be exploitative but it was part of the character development of the script that Lea's character had always said no to Tom's character until a particular and poignant moment.

Pat now explained. "Look, guys, Lea's young (she was twenty-one at the time) and these young girls will say yes about nudity because they want the role. Unless they've done nudity in a film before, they have no idea what it means to be exposed like that around strangers. A lot of them get on the set, freeze, and refuse to do it. Then, you're stuck. I'll tell her she has the part subject to this one thing so she won't feel like she's being exploited. It's not like some cattle call where these girls have to all take off their clothes for the amusement of the producer and director. This is the last step in getting the part and I'm telling you guys this: if she isn't okay with undressing here in the office, she won't do it on the set."

Michael and I were both married and had young children. We had absolutely no interest whatsoever in participating in Pat's plan. We had no objection, however, to Pat doing the proposed meeting, just as long as we didn't have to be there.

"No way, guys. Undressing in front of another woman is nothing like the set. You guys have to be there, too."

I spoke to Robert Cort who laughed before telling me that we needed to do what Pat suggested. After all, she was more experienced at her job than any of us were at ours.

So, the appointed moment came. Michael and I felt like dirty old men and were totally embarrassed for Lea.

Pat watched us fidget with great amusement.

When Lea came in, she was bubbly, happy, and excited. She thanked all of us profusely for believing in her and promised that she would not let us down in the film.

Seeing how uncomfortable we were, Lea said, "Pat explained the situation to me and I completely understand. Don't feel awkward, guys. Really, I'm fine with this."

She then laughed and said, "So, I guess I should take my clothes off now."

And, without batting an eye, she did.

Michael is a real Irishman with the kind of ruddy complexion that turns red very easily. Within seconds, his entire face made Rudolph the Red-nosed Reindeer look pale by comparison. He looked all around the room, every place but at Lea. My face felt as flushed as it did after Harry Cohn had slipped me that shot glass of scotch so I looked down at the floor as much as possible. Until Pat shouted out "Boys, pay attention!"

By that time, Lea had undressed down to her panties and was obviously a lot more comfortable with her nudity than we were.

Michael and I quickly looked up and even more quickly looked away and shouted something like "Yeah, great, thanks, get dressed!"

She dressed, thanked and hugged us all again, and left.

Lea was sensational in the film and went on to have a wonderful career, highlighted by playing Michael J. Fox's mother in the *Back to The Future* films and her own hit television series, *Caroline in the City*.

Michael and I did our best never to talk about that meeting again until I called him to do some fact checking for this book.

I also recently spoke to Pat McCorkle who, I'm happy to report, is busier and more successful than ever at her casting craft. She laughed when recalling our embarrassment and also told me that she has had two other clients over the last several years, both well-known performers, who were as uncomfortable as Michael and I were when they faced similar situations with young actors.

Requiem for An American Steel Town

We shot the film in Johnstown, Pennsylvania in the middle of winter.

At that time, Johnstown had one of the highest unemployment rates of any town in America. The mills had been laying people off for years and the youngest person working in any of the mills that were still operating was around fifty years old. The whole town had an aura of sadness about it. Industrial America was going through a painful downsizing and Johnstown was the epicenter.

Capturing that look was very important to Michael but it was more important for the film that Michael entrust the cinematography to someone else and concentrate on the actors. Michael wisely chose a wonderful Dutchman named Jan DeBont as his cinematographer. Jan later went on to become a director himself (*Speed* and *Twister*).

We wanted the football scenes to be completely realistic so all the actors, including Tom, had agreed to do their own football sequences. We hired Don Yannessa, a legendary high school football coach in Pennsylvania, to train two football teams, including Tom and our actors.

Craig T. Nelson (who had just starred in *Poltergeist*) was cast to play the lead role of a coach in the film.

Craig leaped into his role with great dedication and very soon all the actors were actually referring to Craig as "Coach."

The football action was so realistic that on the first day of filming football practice for the film, Tom had a head-on, helmet-to-helmet collision with Paul Carafotes, who played a character named Salvucci in the film.

They were both knocked out cold.

Fox was something less than thrilled.

Risky Business

Tom had come directly from Chicago, where he had been filming *Risky Business*, to us in Johnstown, and he brought Rebecca de Mornay, with whom he was a having an on and off-camera affair.

Tom's affair with Rebecca made things a bit awkward for Lea, who had to film a nude love scene with Tom. When I gingerly raised that subject to Tom, he and Rebecca responded like consummate pros. Rebecca even left Johnstown while those scenes were being filmed and the love scene went off without a hitch.

The Coach and I

Craig T. Nelson was and is a terrific actor and, when he wasn't drinking, he was also a wonderful man.

Unfortunately, Craig was doing a lot of drinking.

(Another big drinker, W.C.Fields, was at one point supposedly drinking so much that he started to lose his hearing. When his doctor told Fields that he had to either stop drinking or go deaf, Fields got very quiet. When his doctor asked him why he was hesitating, Fields responded: "Lately, what I've been drinking is a whole lot better than what I've been hearing.")

My most memorable moment with Craig occurred one morning around three a.m. when I received a call from the bar at the hotel where Craig and all the actors were staying. I was told that Craig refused to leave the bar until I came to speak to him.

We had rented a house for the shoot that was about fifteen minutes from town. As I drove to the hotel, I was also aware that we had a shooting call in about three hours for the scene in which Craig's character was supposed to throw Tom's character off the team after the team lost a crucial game.

When I arrived, Craig proceeded to harangue me about the importance of winning the game. That the kids could not lose. That they were working way too hard to lose and that they had to get scholarships so they could leave town.

Yes, at that moment, the movie was real and the real was a movie.

He then insisted that his team needed to win the game, not lose it. Which would, of course, have meant changing the entire script. Craig had become so immersed in his method acting that he didn't want to destroy Tom's life by throwing him off the team. He had completely blurred the line between Tom and the character he was playing.

I tried reasoning with him for a while, such as gently pointing out that we had no script for the second half of the film if we did as he suggested.

He, however, remained unconvinced.

Finally, I got exasperated. "Look, Craig, no one has ever paid five dollars to see a Craig T. Nelson movie. Go to your room, get some sleep, and show up and do your damn job."

With that, I left and went home where I didn't even try to go back to sleep.

Amazingly enough, Craig showed up on time and did a brilliant job on the scene.

Michael had some run-ins with Craig as well, including one time when Michael threw Craig up against a wall.

I have to jump ahead here a bit.

Craig called me at home almost a year later. He told me that he had joined Alcoholics Anonymous and that he wanted to make amends with me for all the trouble he had caused during the shoot. His apology was sincere and heartfelt. He truly felt awful about everything. I accepted his apology and wished him well.

Subsequently, Craig publicly discussed his battles with alcohol back then and I learned later from Michael Chapman that Craig had called him as well.

One last postscript.

A few years later, Craig became the star of a huge hit television series entitled *Coach*. Strange coincidence, yes?

I happened to see Craig on a studio lot right around that time.

When I shouted out to him and he recognized me, he put a look of mock terror on his face and pretended to run away while yelling back "Don't blame me. It wasn't my idea!"

With that, we had a wonderful, brief moment together in which he couldn't have been warmer or friendlier.

As I said, he's a really good guy and a terrific actor and I'm happy for all his successes.

Cruise Becomes a Major Star

Risky Business opened in August 1983 and Tom became a huge movie star overnight.

As *All The Right Moves* was set to open just two months later in October, we thought we would benefit enormously from and ride along with Tom's meteoric rise to stardom.

Despite some wonderful reviews from major critics like Roger

Ebert, however, our film never ignited.

Why?

It could have been the R rating as many of Tom's biggest fans at that time were young teenagers. In truth, though, *Risky Business* had been rated R as well.

The biggest issue was, I believe, that our film was a very gritty, realistic look at the plight of young people in very real and desperate situations. As such, it just wasn't as commercial for a mass audience as it needed to be for box office success.

As a filmmaker, though, I had already been through the *Somewhere in Time* box office fiasco, so the results of *All The Right Moves*, while disappointing, were not as devastating.

Regardless of their box office results, I was and still am deeply proud of both films.

CHAPTER ELEVEN

The Lost Years

"You just have to get up every morning, because you never know what the tide is going to bring in."

Cast Away, 2000

The next several years were very difficult professionally but there were two bright spots that I mention only briefly here.

Bill and Ted's Excellent Adventure

My old friend Robert Cort had left Fox soon after I did to join Ted Field's new production company Interscope.

Ted had been the heir to the *Chicago Sun-Times* newspaper and media fortune from Chicago. Unlike most heirs, however, Ted then built on that fortune and became a major player and a highly respected producer in Hollywood.

Ted and Robert had tremendous success together on such films as *Three Men and a Baby, Revenge of the Nerds,* and *Cocktail.*

Very soon after Robert moved to Interscope, I read a hysterically funny script entitled *Bill and Ted's Excellent Adventure* that was co-written by Ed Solomon and Chris Matheson, son of my dear friend Richard.

The writers' agents had reacted so badly to the script that they actually told the writers to throw the script away and start something else. I read it and found it to be one of the funniest and most original scripts I had ever seen.

I submitted it to Robert at Interscope, they bought it immediately, and I met Ted Field for the first time.

Ted asked me about any other projects that I thought he should read and, of course, I gave him *What Dreams May Come*. He was very enthusiastic about the book but thought it was too expensive a project for Interscope to take on at that time.

But I never forgot his interest.

She's Out of Control

In 1986, I sold an amusing little script called *Daddy's Little Girl* to a new company formed by successful producer Jerry Weintraub. The movie centered on a single father's befuddlement at the sudden blossoming of his daughter, a subject matter which I found endearing and knew I would eventually face myself.

Without going into all the details, the film, which starred Tony Danza and Catherine Hicks, was released in 1988 after being retitled *She's Out of Control*.

An adorable young girl named Amy Dolenz (daughter of the famous "Monkee", Mickey Dolenz) played the lead.

The script called for her to have a boy friend, a kid described in the script as being so obnoxious that the father wanted to kill him.

When we auditioned young actors for the part, one stood out above the rest as just about the most obnoxious kid any of us had ever met. In fact, the director Stan Dragoti was so put off by the kid's antics that he wanted to throw him out of the audition.

For some reason, I kind of intuited what the kid was doing and thought that if I was right, the kid had big time courage.

My sense was that he had come into the audition as the obnoxious character that the script called for and had stayed in character the whole time. (Jane Seymour had come to the *Somewhere In Time* audition as her character Elise McKenna and remained in character the whole time. That worked. Why not this?)

I thought that the kid was brave and wonderful, convinced Stan to give him a chance, and we hired him.

Even on the set, he managed to stay in character and find a way to annoy just about everyone, but I was onto him and he knew it. I even confronted him one day with my convictions about his behavior. After a few such encounters, he one day just winked at me, and that was that.

He did a great job in a small part, and Matthew Perry later went on to become quite a star when he joined some other great *Friends*.

CHAPTER TWELVE

In Bed With Madonna

"I'm not bad. I'm just drawn that way."
Who Framed Roger Rabbit?, 1988

My *Kramer vs. Kramer* Moment

In late May 1990, I was bankrupt, desperate, heartbroken, terrified, and in dire need of a job.

My divorce lawyer told me that I better find work or my kids would be taken away from me and raised elsewhere by my soon-to-be-ex-wife's parents.

With two weeks to go until our divorce trial in 1990, I had no job.

Utterly desperate, I turned for help to three friends: Jim Wiatt, who was then the second in command at the huge agency ICM, Ric Nicita at rival agency CAA, and MGM executive Richard Berger.

I explained my predicament to all three of them and, to my eternal gratitude, they immediately coordinated calls to Dino De Laurentiis who was looking for a new production president for his new company after his former company had gone bankrupt.

Dino didn't know it at the time but we certainly had that in common.

For CAA and ICM to have agreed on anything was somewhat akin to the Hatfields inviting the McCoys over for Thanksgiving dinner. Dino was so impressed that such fierce rivals were calling him about the same guy that he hired me on the spot.

My contract was finished literally days before I had to go though my divorce trial, and I didn't have to face the specter of losing my kids.

I drove away from our trial in the L.A. County courthouse in June 1990 and reported for my first day of work with Dino.

And a new life began.

The Real Italian Stallion

Ray Stark and Dino De Laurentiis were the last of the old-time "mogul" producers and it was my great honor to head production for both of them.

Weirdly enough, Dino too had tragically lost a son before I started to work for him.

Two men who had lost sons hired a guy who had lost his father. Freud would have loved us

Dino De Laurentiis was and still is a living legend.

He almost single handedly put the Italian film business on the movie map in the 1940s through the 1960s, producing countless classics such as *La Strada, Nights of Cabiria,* and *Bitter Rice* with directors such as Federico Fellini. Coming to America, he also produced classic films such as *Serpico, Conan The Barbarian,* and *Three Days of The Condor.*

Dino was also a consummate entrepreneur who single-handedly invented the concept of the separate selling of foreign and U.S rights to films. Here's how it worked:

Dino would decide on a project and a budget. He would then pre-sell the distribution rights to the film in the United States and make a separate deal for the rest of the world. Dino's sense of the market was so keen, and his salesmanship was so extraordinary, that he would almost always lock in both a profit and also a big producing fee for himself before filming even began.

For instance, if he was making a film for fifteen million dollars, he would try to pre-sell all rights for at least eighteen million dollars, thus locking in a profit of three million dollars before the film even began shooting. At that point, box office results were somewhat irrelevant but, if the film did do well, Dino would make even more money from his profit participation. He also usually took a one million dollar producing fee from the budget itself, which increased his take in this example to four million dollars.

Going forward, the key to making the model work was keeping the film on budget. Almost all other producers used production bonds on films because their guarantors would step in and cover overages after a certain cushion had been exceeded. Dino, however, hated production bonds because their costs ate into his profits and, furthermore, he could not abide the thought of some bond company taking over control of one of his films.

Dino's split rights financing concept resuscitated and re-birthed the independent film industry and Dino flourished.

Diminutive in physical stature, Dino had the heart of a lion, a symbol that he quite appropriately used as his company logo. And, oh, did Dino love movies. That was something that he and Ray Stark shared: a huge passion for deal making and a love for films and the people who made them.

Dino lived, breathed, and dreamed about movies and it was the experience of a lifetime to share film adventures with him, even at that late moment in his career.

In Bed With Madonna

Early in my tenure with Dino, we made a deal to distribute Madonna's documentary *Truth or Dare* outside the United States.

Ever the salesman, Dino decided to retitle the film *In Bed With Madonna*, and, as a result, Dino's presales exceeded the guarantee that he had made to acquire the film.

Madonna was, at that time, the biggest female star in the world, not just in movies but also in entertainment in general. She was also one of the most famous people in the world.

Dino wanted to make a film with her and had asked her what kind of film she wanted to make. Dino told me that Madonna had immediately responded that she wanted to do a very sexy thriller, ala *Basic Instinct* which had just been giant success and had made Sharon Stone into an overnight star.

Dino told me to find a thriller that we could make with Madonna and to do so very quickly.

I found a script entitled *Body of Evidence* about a femme fatale. Dino loved it, we bought it immediately, Madonna signed on along with a German film director whom she admired named Uli Edel, and we were off to the races. I grew to greatly respect and admire Uli as well.

Dino leaped into action regarding presales and pretty soon we had a domestic deal with MGM and sizable foreign presales. As long as the film came in on budget, Dino stood to clear a significant profit.

That's where I came in and how I finally met Madonna.

It was to be my job to serve as the creative producer on location and make sure that the film stayed on budget. (As to the budget, I was greatly aided by my old friend and mentor Mel Dellar who had by that time become the dean of American line producers.)

It was also my responsibility to assure that Madonna was happy with the whole process and that scared the hell out of me.

Madonna was much more important to the project than I was so I had no idea how I was going to have any kind of leverage with her at all. If she wanted something, how was I going to say no? If her whims took us over budget, I knew Dino wouldn't hesitate to fire me and that was something I couldn't afford to let happen.

To clarify everything, I asked for a meeting with Madonna and went to her house to see her. I had decided to be totally honest with her and basically throw myself at her mercy.

With my heart in my throat, I stammered out something like:

"Look, you're the most famous woman in the world and I'm just a guy at a production company who needs to keep the film on budget and on schedule. I have no way to force you to do anything because we both know that you're a lot more important to the movie than I am. So, with that said, I just need to know directly from you: what do I have to do to make this work for you and also find a way to prevent myself from being fired?"

Her reaction in that moment will forever be etched in my memory.

I was sitting in a chair in her living room and she was sitting on the couch. That is, she had been sitting on the couch.

When I finished my little speech, she jumped up and moved quickly towards me. For an instant, I thought that I had offended her so much that she was going to slap me.

Instead, she came right up to me and, with a smile, gave me a hug.

Rather being angry, she told me that she was utterly delighted with how direct I had been with her. She also told me that all she would ever expect from me was the complete honesty that I had just shared with her.

She went on to say that I had nothing to fear from her, that she understood and respected budgets and schedules, and that we would get along great if she knew she could always count on my being straight with her.

Somewhat stunned, and utterly relieved, I promised that such would be the case and we never had a single problem during the entire shoot.

Madonna was an consummate pro at all times, and became my favorite performer with whom I had ever worked.

Madonna Keeps Her Word

Several opportunities arose to test our new understanding.

We made an offer to the first person that Madonna had requested as her hair stylist for the film. He immediately rejected the offer and demanded more than twice what we had in the budget.

I explained the problem to Madonna who could have easily insisted that I give the guy what he wanted. She was the star and having the hair stylist that would make her the most comfortable would not have been an unreasonable demand.

She, however, told me to tell the guy that our budget was our budget and we could go no higher. I did. He must have thought I was bluffing and wouldn't budge. I told Madonna and she calmly said to go on to her next choice and make it clear up front what we had to spend. I did just that and her second choice became her hair stylist.

Next, there was a moment in which Madonna and our director scheduled a screening of a yet-to-be-released film entitled *The Lovers*.

Studios are hesitant to screen films before they are released but they also often bend that rule when a director asks for a screening, which Uli did. MGM was releasing both our film and *The Lovers*.

Before the screening, Uli had to excuse himself because of another meeting and MGM cancelled the screening altogether.

When her assistant informed Madonna of the cancellation, Madonna was annoyed and asked to speak to me. Deciding to do as she had requested, I explained that the studio had agreed to show the film to Uli, not her.

"Madonna, the truth is that they just don't do this kind of thing except for directors. They don't care if you see it."

She would have had every right to be offended, stamp her feet, or make a scene. Instead, she just calmly said "Oh, OK. Thanks for telling me the truth. I understand." And that was the end of that.

Madonna Swats The S.W.A.T Squad

With Madonna, not only did she have an utter lack of airs and movie star ego, she also had an impish sense of humor.

For instance, she teased me a lot about what she was going to say to my daughters when she first met them, but when they actually did visit the set, she couldn't have been any kinder.

There was one area, however, where Madonna was totally adamant.

She was a fitness fanatic at that time and she made it clear to me that we needed to schedule time so that she could do her workouts, some of which included long runs on the city streets of Portland, Oregon, where we shot all of the exteriors of the film.

There was no way that we could have Madonna out there running alone and so we had to hire security guards for her.

The head of our security was Pete Weireter who was actually one the training instructors for the Los Angeles Police Department.

Pete met Madonna and mistakenly underestimated her strength and stamina. He was even more mistaken to have intimated to Madonna that he was very sure that his guys could do the job.

Madonna took Pete's overconfidence as a personal challenge and told me with a knowing smile that their first morning run together would be most amusing.

Sure enough, she took off the next morning and eventually left her entire security squad in her wake.

She came back.

None of them did.

Pete had to send out a car to pick up the stragglers and, from that moment on, a car always accompanied Madonna on her runs.

A few years, Pete later gained international notoriety as the LAPD official who was on the phone with OJ Simpson and Al Cowlings during the infamous White Bronco low-speed chase and surrender. He also tried his hand at acting and can be seen onscreen as the police negotiator at the beginning and end of the film *Bandits*, with Bruce Willis, Billy Bob Thornton, and Cate Blanchett.

Making Madonna Cry

Body of Evidence includes some steamy sex between Madonna and Willem Dafoe but the set was closed for those scenes. For me, the most memorable moment of the shoot actually occurred on a courtroom set that we had built in Los Angeles.

The scene called for Madonna to be vulnerable and cry while she was testifying on the witness stand. After a few takes, it became evident that Madonna was having difficulty getting herself into a place where she felt she could cry.

After a few more unsuccessful attempts, the actor playing the District Attorney in the film took me aside.

Joe Mantegna was a pro's pro, a consummate actor who always showed up, hit his lines with talent and enthusiasm, and was a pleasure to be around.

We all admired Joe immensely, and so did Madonna. Joe and Madonna had previously appeared together on Broadway in David Mamet's *Speed the Plow* and she had remarked to several of us how much she liked and respected Joe.

Joe whispered to me that he knew he could help Madonna in the scene but he didn't want to step on the toes of the director. I went to Uli who was always open to suggestions and had none of the directorial ego flights that some of his brethren inflicted on others.

I brought a very willing Uli over to Joe who told Uli to keep the cameras rolling on the next take, no matter what happened.

My sister Susie and brother-in-law Jim just happened to be visiting me on the set that day so I went over to warn them about what was about to happen. I couldn't warn the entire crew, however, without calling too much attention and ruining the moment for Joe and Madonna.

Two notes here to set up what happened next:

First, there were two cameras rolling and both of them were focused only on Madonna. One camera angle was a medium shot of her and the other was an extreme close-up.

Second, Joe Mantegna is one of the most courtly, thoughtful, and polite guys you would ever want to meet.

When Uli yelled "action" for the next take, Joe was standing just behind the camera and only a very few feet from Madonna.

Suddenly, Joe started screaming at and berating Madonna in the most shocking manner you could imagine. He used every epithet and every insult that anyone could ever have thought of, and then some. He impugned her integrity, her acting ability, her looks, and everything else he could think of.

As the camera was on Madonna, he knew his off-screen voice could be edited out.

The crew was transfixed.

After a couple of minutes, Madonna's tears began to flow.

When Uli finally yelled "Cut!" to our stunned crew, Joe went up and hugged Madonna, and she, in turn, thanked him profusely.

I would venture to say that Joe was one of the few people to ever scream insults at Madonna and get a hug in return.

AKA The Antichrist

After we had finished production (on time and on budget), and after we had a couple of decent, if not stellar previews, Madonna's explicit coffee table book *Sex* was published and her album *Erotica* was released.

The critical response to the album and book were very negative and MGM, which was releasing *Body of Evidence* in the United States, became very concerned about Madonna's image.

Alan Ladd, Jr., who was the head of MGM at the time, came up with the very smart idea of going back to the same theater (I think it was in Seattle, but I'm not sure) where we had staged a fairly successful preview a couple of months before.

Same theater, same audience make-up.

The idea was to see if perceptions of Madonna had changed.

The new preview was fairly disastrous in that the positive response to the film dropped precipitously from the earlier preview.

In reading the preview cards, it became apparent that the primary cause of the different scores was that the audience image of Madonna had changed dramatically.

The film opened in early 1993 to bad reviews and weak box office.

After the film was released, I asked Madonna to personally sign two posters for me.

On the first, she simply said "To Stephen, Love, Madonna."

On the second, which still hangs in our house, she wrote:

"For Stephen. With love, Madonna, AKA the Anti-Christ."

Getting Fired, Again

After almost three years with Dino, a few things had become very clear to me.

First, the entire era of Old Hollywood was coming to an end. The corporate takeover of Hollywood was almost complete. Things were changing rapidly and not for the better.

Second, it had also become clear that I was just not a very good studio executive.

In my heart, I was a producer with a passion for a particular niche of films that were inspiring and uplifting, not for general audience films. I just couldn't bring myself to champion a project anymore because I thought a general audience might like the film. I wanted to feel excited enough myself about a project to see it through from development to release, not watch others go off to make films.

Third, as a result of my rapidly waning interest in the executive aspects of my job, it was obvious that the end of my time with Dino was drawing near.

I wanted to make more positive, uplifting films and not be so completely focused on presales, etc. Dino wanted to continue to do what he had always done; that is, find and fund commercial films, regardless of their nature.

I understood and respected that and him.

I just couldn't find it in my heart to go along anymore.

The actual end came swiftly.

In 1992, Dino wanted to be in business with Ron Bass, who was the hottest writer in Hollywood. Ron had won an Academy Award for *Rainman*, had also written the smash hit *Sleeping with The Enemy*, and had development deals all over town.

Ron and I had first met and become friendly while Ron was still practicing law in 1979. He had been Christopher Reeve's lawyer when we negotiated the deal for *Somewhere in Time*. Ron and I had always talked about working together but had not yet been able to do so.

At Dino's request, I asked Ron to come meet with us and pitch something to Dino that we could develop together. Ron had heard all sorts of stories about Dino, but he was curious to meet him and so he agreed to come in for a meeting.

Before the meeting, I warned Dino that Ron was getting seven hundred and fifty thousand dollars (or around that) for an original first draft and a set of revisions. Dino was unaccustomed to paying that kind of money to screenwriters for an original idea but was undeterred.

Ron pitched an idea for a vampire film that he had always wanted to write, Dino jumped at the chance to say yes, and we made a deal.

A few months later, Ron submitted the first draft and Dino absolutely hated it.

I mean, he really hated it. Dino felt that Ron had not delivered the story that he had pitched to us. He was, in fact, so apoplectically angry about it that he told me that he wanted to cancel the deal altogether, get back the initial money we had paid Ron up front, and not pay the remaining balance.

I explained to Dino that we had a written contract with Ron and there was no way that we could get out of it. As to the story itself, I firmly believed that Ron had indeed delivered the script that he had pitched. The first draft wasn't great but it was, after all, simply a first draft. That's what rewrites are all about.

Dino told me to call Ron and voice his displeasure, which I did.

Ron responded like the pro that he was by saying he would come get our notes, and do as significant a revision as Dino requested.

Before the meeting, I told Dino that Ron was amenable to a complete rewrite at our instructions.

Dino was, however, fixated on getting out of the deal. I told Dino that we couldn't just cancel the deal, and that I wouldn't be party to trying to get out of it. He then told me that it was my job to do what he told me to do. (To be fair to Dino here, he really did believe that Ron had failed to deliver the story he had pitched; therefore, even though I disagreed with his conclusion, Dino felt that he was legally entitled to rescind the deal.)

Ron came in and couldn't have been more gracious. He told Dino that he wanted Dino to be happy with the script and that he would tear it apart and basically start again from scratch if Dino so desired.

Dino, however, wanted out and told Ron that he had not delivered the story that he had pitched and that Dino felt he should get a refund and not have to pay the balance of the fee that was still due.

Ron was shocked but kept his cool, apologized again for disappointing Dino, and again said he would make whatever changes Dino wanted. Ron also gently, but firmly, told Dino that he had indeed delivered the story that he had pitched. I think he even offered to settle with Dino for half of what his contract called for but Dino wasn't interested.

At that point, both Dino and Ron turned to look at me.

Dino wanted his employee to support his position.

Ron was just looking for some sort of guidance as to how to proceed.

The great French philosopher Francois Voltaire supposedly once attended an orgy. When he was invited to attend another one, he declined by saying "Absolutely not. Once a philosopher, twice a pervert."

Orgy aside, that's exactly where I felt that I was in the moment.

Years before, I hadn't spoken up during the Stark/Nancy Meyers/*Freestyle* fiasco. I had sat by and rationalized other behavior as well during those years and knew that I just couldn't do it again.

So, I very clearly stated that I thought Ron was right, that Dino was wrong, and that we should honor the deal that we had made.

Dino stood and abruptly ended the meeting.

As we walked out of Dino's office, Ron asked me what I thought he should do and I just told him to sit tight and see what happened. Dino often got upset about things only to relent later.

As he left, Ron told me that he hoped I would be all right.

I already knew that I wasn't.

A few minutes later, I was summoned back into Dino's office and he fired me on the spot. He told me that it was my job to support him and the company, not my friends, and that he no longer trusted me enough to continue to work with me.

Dino believed he was right about Ron and had every right to expect me to behave in the way he had demanded; however, I didn't agree with Dino's assessment and just couldn't acquiesce to it.

Within a week, we had negotiated a settlement to my contract and I was gone.

The Last Moguls

Working with Dino turned out to be my last executive job.

Unlike what had happened with Ray, I deeply regret that I never had a rapprochement with Dino.

Dino and Ray were the last of The Old Hollywood mogul producers.

It was an honor for me to have worked for them both.

CHAPTER THIRTEEN

What Dreams and Nightmares May Come

"Never give up. Never give up. Never give up."
"Too much persistence can be kind of stupid."
What Dreams May Come, 1998

Albert Einstein once said that the definition of insanity is doing the same thing over and over again and expecting a different result.

There's also a quote from an old movie (the title of which I have long since forgotten): "Fools are the only ones who accomplish the impossible because they're the only ones who try."

This chapter (both in this book and in my life) spans a twenty year time period that illuminates that fine line between persistence and lunacy.

It also starts in The Old Hollywood and ends in The New Hollywood.

My strange two decade odyssey to produce *What Dreams May Come* bridges the transition between the two Hollywoods and also is an example of the kind of insanity that fools like me embrace when we become obsessed with getting a film made.

In other words, "Momma, don't let your babies grow up to be film producers."

The Odyssey Begins

While we were in preproduction on *Somewhere In Time*, Richard Matheson gave me the galleys to his new novel *What Dreams May Come*.

I was absolutely transfixed by the book because it was then, and still remains, one of the most imaginative and poignant love stories ever.

Dreams is the story of a man who dies and then descends through the pit of hell to find his wife. It's a story that takes place almost exclusively in the afterlife experience of the main characters.

After my first meeting with Richard Matheson in 1976, it had taken three years for me to get *Somewhere In Time* produced. As confident and deluded as ever, I swore to Richard that it wouldn't take three years to get *What Dreams May Come* produced.

And I was right.

It took Ulysses ten years to get home from The Trojan War.

It took me twenty years just to get a film made.

As I said, a genius I'm not.

Somewhere In Time Bombs

Despite Michael Douglas' sage advice, my first assumption had been that *Somewhere In Time* was going to be a huge hit that would then open a clear pathway to get someone to develop *What Dreams May Come*.

Unfortunately, an avalanche obliterated that imaginary pathway when *Somewhere In Time* bombed.

You Can't Do That On Film

Over the years, I submitted the book to almost every director in the world whom I thought could actually translate it to the screen but they all passed.

For example, I am a huge fan of Peter Weir's work, particularly his early Australian films *Picnic at Hanging Rock* and *The Last Wave*. Later, he directed such fascinating films as *The Truman Show*.

After submitting the book to him, I received a call from Weir saying that he loved the book but had no idea how to put it on screen.

I heard that a lot from several directors for many years.

And so it went.

Until…

Steven Spielberg is On The Phone

In late 1982, I was prepping *All The Right Moves* at Fox when my assistant came into my office and said someone was calling me from Steven Spielberg's office.

Right. And Jimmy Hoffa wanted to meet me for lunch.

Although I knew that I would pick up the phone to find one of my less-than-clever friends on the line, I decided to go along.

When I picked up the phone, it was actually Richard Matheson.

"Stephen, I'm sitting here in Steven Spielberg's office at Warner Brothers. He' s very interested in *What Dreams May Come*. Can you come over here right now?"

Nah, I don't want to drive to the Valley. There's so much traffic, and.. ARE YOU KIDDING ME?

I left my office so fast that I made Wil. E. Coyote look like a turtle.

While I flew up the 405 (San Diego Freeway) to the San Fernando Valley, my mind was racing.

Although I hadn't heard from Richard in a while, I remembered that he had been asked by Spielberg to write a screenplay for a segment that Spielberg was going to direct for *The Twilight Zone* movie.

Richard had been one of the main writers on the original *Twilight Zone* series. He had also written the screenplay for *Duel*, which had turned out to be Spielberg's first feature film as a director.

Richard and I had sent *What Dreams May Come* to Spielberg a long time before but had never heard a response.

I also knew that Spielberg was very keen on doing a remake of an old film called *A Guy Named Mike* that was itself an afterlife love story so I had just assumed he had no interest in *Dreams*.

Spielberg's In, Unless He Isn't

When I arrived at Spielberg's office, I was ushered right in.

Although I had never met Spielberg before, he couldn't have been nicer or more collegial.

He told us both that he had indeed read *Dreams* some time ago but could not bring himself to get involved or call us.

When Richard asked why not, Spielberg told us that he and (actress) Amy Irving (whom he had been dating) had read the book together and that it was a very emotional experience for both of them.

They broke up a little time later and Spielberg said he just couldn't focus on the book because of the break-up. (They eventually got back together again and married in 1985.)

Spielberg told us that he was fascinated by the book and complimented Richard for having created a device in the story that no other afterlife story that he had ever read contained.

When we both asked him what he meant, he responded:

"Jeopardy. That's what's missing from most afterlife stories. If you're dead, where's the jeopardy that propels the film forward? *Dreams* solves that by having the main character search for his wife and put his soul in danger. That's why I'm so intrigued by it."

Could this really be happening?

Spielberg had just directed *E.T.*, which had become the biggest box office film ever to date.

Was he really going to commit to *Dreams*?

He explained that he did indeed want to develop a script with Richard. He was already committed to directing a segment of The *Twilight Zone Movie* and said he was then going to direct *Indiana Jones and The Temple of Doom*.

If the script for *Dreams* worked out, he said he could direct it after *Doom*. (From *Doom* to *Dreams*. Quite an arc.)

He then turned to me and said in a very friendly way that he already had producers that he worked with and that they would have to be part of the deal. He quickly added, however, that he would be more than happy to have me be one of the producers on the film.

Just having a producing credit of any kind on a Spielberg film would have been a huge boost to my career so his proposal was more than fine with me.

He then said that we should make the development deal either with Warners or Universal and asked me if I had a preference.

When I responded that I had an exclusive producing deal with Fox, the mood in the room shifted.

He told me that he had no interest or intention of working at Fox. When I asked him why, he replied that he had nothing against Fox but he had worked with Norman Levy before and did not want to do so again.

Uh-oh.

Spielberg had obviously earned the right to make whatever movies he wanted to make at any studio that he preferred. He had strong relationships at Warners and Universal and wanted to work where he felt the most comfortable. I, however, had that exclusive deal with Fox and Norman Levy was my mentor and friend.

The meeting ended with Spielberg saying very politely that I needed to decide how to proceed. We shook hands and I left.

To Spielberg or not to Spielberg, That Was The Question

As soon as I arrived back at Fox, I went right to Norman's office. Norman was then the Vice-Chairman of the whole studio with a particular focus on distribution, which was his area of expertise. Around that time, he had hired a young executive named Tom Sherak to make day-to-day distribution decisions. Today, Tom is the President of the Academy of Motion Picture Arts and Sciences.

Norman was one of the warmest, kindest people I had known in the industry. He had always been absolutely wonderful to me, both at Columbia where we first met, and now at Fox. If anyone in my career could ever have been described as my "Dutch uncle", it would have been Norman Levy.

When I explained the whole situation to Norman, he got as pale as a ghost. Spielberg was the number one director in the industry and the fact that he refused to work with Norman was devastating news to my friend. If he could possibly avoid it, he certainly didn't want his boss Marvin Davis to hear anything about this situation so he asked me to sit tight for a while and I agreed.

Fairly quickly, I was summoned back to Norman's office.

Norman had tried to call Spielberg with no success but he had found out from some mutual friends that Speilberg's issue with Norman stemmed from the Columbia days and certain things that had happened several years earlier on *Close Encounters of The Third Kind*, which Spielberg had directed and Norman had distributed.

Norman asked me to take one more shot at convincing Spielberg to at least talk to Norman.

I called Spielberg who continued to be friendly but adamant about his position, which seemed to be more about his positive feelings about Universal and Warner Brothers than his negative feelings about Norman.

At that point, I thought I had no other option than to call Richard and tell him that he should make the deal with Spielberg without me.

Fox did not own any rights to the book itself and, although I didn't want to lose the project, I also couldn't stand in Richard's way of having Steven Spielberg direct the film.

Richard, however, told me that he did not want to do the project without me. I was so deeply touched by that, then and now. That is vintage Richard Matheson. Classy, loving, kind, and loyal.

I went to see Norman again and he said that he needed to tell Marvin Davis what was going on.

George Lucas and a Life-Changing Decision

I was then brought into a meeting with Norman, Marvin Davis, and Joe Wizan, the new head of production at Fox.

Fox had distributed the first two *Star Wars* films and was about to release the third, *Return of the Jedi*. Marvin knew that George Lucas and Spielberg were very close friends so Marvin called Lucas, explained what was going on with Spielberg and *Dreams*, and asked if Lucas would consider calling Spielberg on Fox's behalf. Lucas asked to see the book first and Marvin had one couriered to him that day.

A few days later, I was summoned back to Davis' office.

From the minute I walked in, I saw from the look on Norman Levy's haggard and worried face that something was very amiss.

Marvin explained that Lucas had read the book, thought it was fascinating (and told Marvin so), and did indeed call Spielberg. Lucas then called Marvin to tell him that Spielberg was indeed adamant about making the *Dreams* deal at either Warners or Universal.

Joe Wizan had read the book too by then and told Marvin in my presence that he agreed with Lucas: a Spielberg movie adapting that book could be one of the great movies ever. (Joe's response was the first time any executive anywhere had seen in the book what I had always seen so he became my favorite executive.)

Looking pained in the extreme, Norman told me that Fox had decided to exempt *Dreams* from my exclusive deal with Fox.

He went on to say that they could not in good faith prevent me from producing the film elsewhere with Spielberg and that I was free to do so. (Let me just throw in here that they absolutely could have prevented me from doing so as many, if not most, other studios would have done. To allow me that freedom was an incredibly gracious act.)

Norman quickly added that they wanted me to at least consider an alternative: Fox would purchase the book from Matheson and promise me that they would find another director to develop and then make the film.

Of course, that meant I had to say no to Steven Spielberg.

The meeting ended and I wandered back to my office in a complete daze.

I called Richard and told him what had happened. Rather than being anxious, he was actually quite amused. He told me that I was the producer and the decision was up to me. Whatever I decided to do was fine with him.

What to do?

On the one hand, working with Spielberg was an off the charts opportunity. Spielberg was and still is a beyond brilliant director. Having him direct *Dreams* could have been utterly magical; moreover, receiving a producing credit on a Spielberg film could have been the jumpstart for my producing career that I had thought *Somewhere In Time* was going to be.

I also felt an enormous responsibility to Richard Matheson to put the project in the best possible situation for it to be a success.

On the other hand, Norman Levy was my friend and mentor. This situation had been incredibly humiliating for him with Marvin Davis. Norman and Fox had been wonderful to me. They had made a great producing deal with me even though *Somewhere In Time*, my only producing credit to date, had bombed. And we were about to get into production on *All the Right Moves*.

I also had the strong sense that Fox's offer to let me go had been engineered by Norman. He knew what a Spielberg movie would mean to my career and he wasn't going to let his own failed relationship with Spielberg stop me. Again, that kind of decency was and is rare in Hollywood, Old and New.

I had already destroyed a relationship with one mentor (Ray Stark). Was I willing to do that again?

I also knew that the deal with Spielberg would only be to develop the book into a script. Spielberg had lots of other projects and there was no guarantee that he would ever direct *Dreams*.

Ultimately, I decided to stay at Fox.

Saying No to Spielberg

I told Richard first and he was completely at peace with my decision.

I then called Spielberg and he was extremely gracious as well.

I then told Norman Levy and he responded like a man who had just received a pardon a few minutes prior to his execution. Although Norman had not in any way tried to pressure me to stay at Fox, I could tell that he had really been through the wringer over the Spielberg situation so he was relieved and gratified that I had decided to stay at Fox.

Joe Wizan told me that he thought I had made the right personal decision and that he would work with me to find the right director for the project. He added, however, that, from a professional standpoint, I would have to live from that point forward with the knowledge that I had rejected an opportunity to work with Steven Spielberg.

He sure got that right.

Looking back now, have I ever questioned my decision?

Of course I have. To deny so would simply be foolish.

Could that have been the dumbest professional decision of my life?

Of course it could have been.

The good news and the bad news is that I'll never know.

We never know how our lives would have been changed if we had chosen a different fork in the road so I try my best not to "should" on myself. (And I am very proud of the version of *Dreams* that Vincent Ward eventually and brilliantly directed.)

To look at the bright side, at least I never gave the book to James Cameron (*Titanic, Avatar*) and then turned him down, too. What a bonehead parlay that would have been. Cameron is a great visualist and a great storyteller.

Come to think of it, why didn't I think of Cameron back then?

OK. Enough. As the old saying goes "If my uncle had a couple of less body parts, he'd be my aunt." But he doesn't, so he's my uncle and he'll never be my aunt.

I didn't know it at the time but it would take me another fifteen years to get *Dreams* produced.

The Neverending Story

Fox quickly purchased the book from Matheson but a director search was put on hold because I had *All The Right Moves* to produce in 1983.

After finishing *Moves*, we started the director search in earnest.

In early 1984, Fox had begun production on a science fiction film entitled *Enemy Mine* but had to shut the film down to change directors. They hired a German director named Wolfgang Petersen who had directed both an extraordinary action film about submarines entitled *Das Boot (The Boat)* and also the film adaptation of *The Neverending Story*.

Enemy Mine would be Wolfgang's first film to be shot in English and the executives at Fox were so impressed with Wolfgang that they suggested that we consider him for *Dreams*.

I had seen *Das Boot* and they got a print of *The Neverending Story* for me to see. I was dazzled by the sheer drama of the former and the vision and warmth of the latter.

In addition, after having pursued *Dreams* for about five years at that point, I thought there was something quite poetic about hiring the director of *The Neverending Story*.

We sent him the book to read.

We Have Our Director, Until We Don't

Wolfgang loved the book and, after meeting him in Los Angeles at Fox where he had come for meetings on *Enemy Mine*, Richard and I thought he was the perfect choice.

In an eerie coincidence reminiscent of Spielberg and Amy Irving, Wolfgang had read the book with his wife Maria and wanted to do the film as a testament to her.

We made the deal with Wolfgang and had several meetings with him, including a trip to Munich where he was filming *Enemy Mine* with Dennis Quaid and Lou Gossett, Jr.

Everything was perfect.

Until everything fell apart at the same time.

In 1985, Marvin Davis sold Fox and as is usual in such a case, all the major executives at Fox were fired, including Norman Levy and Joe Wizan.

When a new executive team takes over a studio, all bets are off on projects that were put in the pipeline by the previous regime. Incoming executives usually see such projects as no-win scenarios. If the new regime embraces a project from the old regime and the film succeeds, the lions' share of the credit goes to the old regime. If such a film fails, the new regime is faulted for having gone ahead with it; hence, making an old regime's film is a classic lose/lose scenario for a new regime.

The new management at Fox had absolutely no interest in *What Dreams May Come*, nor did they have any real interest in keeping me around. I was Norman's "guy", Norman was gone, and so, Stephen, there's the door. Don't let it hit you on the way out.

Then Wolfgang withdrew from *Dreams* as well.

Enemy Mine had fizzled and Wolfgang wanted to reassess where he would go next. (Wolfgang went on to make some terrific films such as *The Perfect Storm* and I have always thought very highly of him, both personally and professionally.)

Dreams was put into what's called "turnaround" by Fox; that is, Fox formally rejected it.

To complete the trifecta in 1985, ABC rejected a huge, eighteen hour miniseries that Richard and I been developing together. Richard had written a seven hundred page "bible" for the project to no avail.

I felt awful that I had let Richard Matheson down.

As we had just absorbed some pretty major body blows, Richard and I drifted apart for a few years and *Dreams* lay dormant on the shelf.

Resurrecting *Dreams*

After Dino fired me in 1993, Ron Bass called to voice his support. Even though I told him that my time with Dino was coming to an end anyway and that Ron was in no way responsible for what had happened, he still felt badly. Ever the mensche, he told me that he owed me a favor and that he still wanted us to develop a project together.

And a little light bulb went on above my head.

I told Ron I had an idea but that I needed to do something first before I could discuss it with him.

I then called Richard Matheson and, heart in mouth, and hat in hand, I went to see him.

After stumbling around for a few minutes, I told Richard that I thought we might be able to revive *Dreams* if I could talk Ron Bass into writing a new script. Richard had written a brilliant and visionary story. Ron was so good with dialogue and characters that I thought the combination could catapult us into a new chance for the project.

Richard was his usual magnanimous self and simply said he would support me in whatever I thought should be done. There are very few, if any, writers of Richard's stature who would have been as gracious as he was to me, then and always.

I went home, called Ron, and asked him, no, I begged him, to consider writing the adaptation for *What Dreams May Come*.

Ron read the book right away and called to say that, while he loved it, he thought that the subject matter was so controversial that it was going to be next to impossible to get a studio to pay him to adapt it.

I begged him to give me one shot at a studio. He agreed and we set up a meeting in 1994 at MGM.

Miraculously, they said yes in 1994.

So, after almost fifteen years, the project was set up again.

Until, again, it wasn't.

Fired More Times Than a *Celebrity Apprentice*

Due to prior commitments, we had to wait almost a year for Ron to write the first draft of the script for *Dreams*. During that year, I met and formed a new producing partnership with a writer named Barnet Bain and we also became great friends and collaborators.

When Ron did submit the script to *Dreams*, I was dazzled. His first draft is still the best first draft of a script that I have ever read.

When we had pitched the project to MGM, Ron and I noticed someone in the office as we left the building. Ron recognized him as a New Zealand director named Vincent Ward and Vincent sort of stuck in my mind from that point forward. Vincent had directed an extraordinarily visionary film entitled *Map of The Human Heart* and he seemed just the right person to direct *Dreams*.

When we first submitted Ron's script to Vincent, he passed on it because he could not figure out how to visualize it on screen, After a couple of weeks, however, he called back to say that he thought he had figured it out. We met with him and he described for us the world of wet paint that would ultimately form the basis for the afterlife in *Dreams*.

So, now we had a director and a script that we believed in. Unfortunately, by that time, MGM was no longer in a strong enough financial condition to finance the film and we found ourselves in turnaround hell yet again.

One Last Chance

At that point, both Ron and Vincent were represented by the Creative Artists Agency (CAA), which was the most powerful agency in Hollywood. When MGM put *Dreams* in turnaround, CAA sent the script to every possible financing entity in Hollywood.

I knew that this was our last chance.

I was holding on in Hollywood by my fingernails. If everyone passed again, I feared that the film and I would disappear forever.

That's when my old *Bill and Ted* friend Ted Field showed up.

Ted had always liked the book and he was actually trying to develop another film with Vincent Ward.

We met with Ted and he promised us that he would get Polygram, with whom he had a producing arrangement, to finance the film.

And he did.

After almost eighteen years, the film was actually going to get made.

Robin Williams signed on to play the lead, Annabella Sciorra was cast as his wife, and Cuba Gooding, Jr. came on to play a guide in the afterlife who was also Robin's son in the film.

Working with Cuba on his first film after winning the Academy Award for *Jerry Maguire* was a complete delight. Cuba was friendly, warm, loving, and completely the person you would have hoped he would be, other than his slightly disconcerting preference to shed his clothes at any time and any place. Which he did, in the hotel pool the night before we started shooting the film.

Heaven and Hell

To go back to another Eagles' line from "Hotel California":

"This could be heaven or this could be hell."

The production period of *Dreams* was both.

To accurately chronicle the dramas, challenges, and personality clashes that happened during the filing of *Dreams* would fill a book all by itself so I will leave that to another time and place.

Gay Hendricks

The post-production period on *Dreams* was also littered with tension and disagreement, including several days of re-shooting.

When all was said and done, though, we had a film about which we were all very proud.

Just prior to the release of *Dreams*, I met Gay Hendricks at a party.

I had heard of Gay and his extraordinary wife Kathlyn (Katie) because of their amazing books, including *The Corporate Mystic* and *Conscious Loving*.

Gay and I immediately connected on a multitude of levels and determined right away that we needed to find a way to work together. Although Gay and Katie were kind enough to invest in the production company that Barnet and I had formed, my most exciting adventure with the Hendricks wouldn't happen until 2004 when we started The Spiritual Cinema Circle together (Chapter Sixteen).

Gay became the person who resurrected my career and forever changed the way I looked at business, relationships, and the world itself.

The Oscar

Dreams went on to be nominated for two 1999 Academy Awards and won the Oscar for Best Visual Effects. I have always believed that Annabella Sciorra also deserved at least a nomination for her brilliant and harrowing portrayal of Robin's wife in the film.

Commercially, the film grossed over one hundred million dollars worldwide but was still considered a flop in Hollywood because it never recouped its almost ninety million dollar production cost and substantial ad budget.

When the film was released in October 1998, the reviews were pretty savage.

But not all of them.

Gene Siskel

I first met Gene Siskel (later of Siskel and Ebert and their ubiquitous thumbs up) in 1965 when he was at Yale and I was at The University of Pennsylvania. I have no memory now of the circumstances of that meeting but we became friendly and stayed in touch with each other from time to time from that point forward.

Gene became a film critic and in the mid 1970s, he teamed up with fellow critic Roger Ebert to host a show called *Sneak Preview*, which was eventually syndicated across the country.

I remember being elated that I had a friend who had become a nationally recognized film critic. I thought that Gene would be the one critic who would always give any film I was involved with the benefit of the doubt. (Other than my wonderful sister, of course, but she always, and quite correctly, had to print a disclaimer about my films and even she wasn't too crazy about some of them.)

Gene, however, panned every single film I ever produced.

It got so bad that Roger Ebert actually noted it when Gene dissed *All The Right Moves* even though Roger really liked it.

When Gene and I spoke or saw each other, we laughed about it. Actually, he laughed and I pretended to be a good sport.

I last saw him in New York in 1993 after the screenings of *Body of Evidence*, which I knew he would rip apart. When I ran into him in a hallway there, he just looked at me and shook his head in disgust.

I'll never forget that exchange.

"Gene, are you ever going to give me a good review?"

"Stephen, are you ever going to make a good movie?"

Fade out.

When *Dreams* was released in 1998, Gene had already been receiving treatment for a cancerous brain tumor.

I had been crestfallen at some of the early reviews for the film. I dreaded even reading Gene's review but I couldn't stop myself. To my complete shock, Gene (and Roger) gave the film the two best reviews that it received from the national media.

Gene, in fact, gave us the lead quote for all our ads: "One of the great achievements in film history."

I tried to reach Gene but couldn't. A few months later, I was deeply saddened to hear that he had died.

I truly hope that Gene actually enjoyed the film as a film even though I can't help feeling that he might have experienced it less as a film than as a glimpse of what lay ahead of him on his own personal journey.

I can only hope that it gave him hope and peace of mind.

One Of The Most Expensive Indie Films Ever

I am deeply proud of *Dreams* and I also understand why the film was not commercially successful enough to turn a profit. As a friend once told me, "Stephen, *What Dreams May Come* is one of the most expensive indie (independent) films ever made."

What he meant by that was that the film was way too challenging and controversial to be a mainstream success; however, because of the stars and budget, it had to be sold that way. And he was absolutely correct.

As it was with *Somewhere In Time* and *All The Right Moves*, time continues to be kind to *Dreams* as more and more people experience it on cable and DVD.

My wife Lauren has a wonderful phrase that applies here as well:

"I have come to believe that we don't find great films. They find us."

On a completely different level, I was about to learn that the intangibles of the *Dreams* experience far outweighed everything else.

"Life All Comes Down To A Few Moments.
This Is One Of Them."

Charlie Sheen uttered that great line in *Wall Street*.

I was about to experience one of those moments.

When *Dreams* opened in 1998, I was made aware of a father in Wisconsin who had a terminally ill seventeen-year old daughter who wanted badly to see the film but was too ill to get to a theater.

We had a courier deliver a videotape to her father and I left him a message on his answering machine.

A couple of weeks later, he called back and we had a conversation that changed my life.

Charles (Chuck) Weber was and still is a basement contractor in Milwaukee, Wisconsin. In 1998, his daughter Amanda was dying of cancer when she saw some television ads for *What Dreams May Come*.

Although she was confined to a bed in their living room and was much too ill to attend a theater, she desperately wanted to see the film. Chuck contacted a local theater owner who in turn contacted Polygram who in turn contacted me. Fortunately, my old friend Andrew Fogelson was the President of Polygram in the United States at that time. He cut through all the corporate red tape so we could get a video copy of the film run off and sent to Wisconsin.

When the film was delivered, Chuck invited a few of Amanda's friends and, together, they watched the film. Except for Chuck.

"I have to tell you, Stephen, I really didn't watch the movie. I watched Amanda watch the movie. When the whole painted world sequence was over, I saw Amanda relax in a way I had not seen before. When the film was over, and we were alone, she told me that she was at peace. When I asked her why, she referred to the painted world in the film and simply said 'Dad, when I die, that's where I'll be.'"

Chuck then paused a moment.

"The next day, she asked to be taken out to a park to see the fall colors because they so reminded her of the sequences in your film. The day after that, she died very peacefully. So, Stephen, I just want to say something to you. I have no idea how this film is doing at the box office and I have no idea what the critics think about it. Frankly, I don't care about either one and neither should you. This film changed the last two days of my daughter's life and that's the only kind of success that should ever matter to you."

For one of the few times in my life, I was speechless.

I also soon came to learn that Amanda had a wicked sense of humor. Chuck had her ashes sculpted into two beautiful crystal balls, one of which I am deeply honored to have in our home. On the stand that holds the crystalline structure, Amanda had her father inscribe:

Amanda A. Weber

1981-1998

"I told you I was sick."

Everything shifted for me that day in 1998 because of the courage and inspiration of Amanda and Chuck Weber.

I knew then that my career in Hollywood was as good as over and that my life was about to change again.

Forever.

CHAPTER FOURTEEN

Checking Out of the Hotel California

"You can check out any time you like,
but you can never leave."
"Hotel California" by Glenn Frey, Don Henley, and Don Felder, 1977

Although I hung around for another couple of years, it had become clear to me that there was no place for me in Hollywood any longer. Old or New.

For the reasons I will detail in Chapter Fifteen, the Old Hollywood that I had grown up around and worked in for so long was gone.

As I had barely survived in the Old Hollywood, I knew that I had no prospects in The New Hollywood.

So, in 2001, I left California forever and moved to Oregon.

What has transpired over the last nine years is beyond the scope of this book so I will just briefly repeat what I said in my introduction to this book.

The move to Oregon changed everything for me.

All my dreams became manifest only after I checked out of the Hotel California.

All but one: the rebirth of The Old Hollywood. Not just in California, but all around the world.

As to that dream, it turns out that the Eagles were absolutely right.

I had checked out.

But I could never really leave.

CHAPTER FIFTEEN

How Old Hollywood Became New Hollywood ...and Why It's in So Much Trouble

"I was just thinking what an interesting concept it is to eliminate the writer from the artistic process. If we could just get rid of these actors and directors, maybe we've got something here."

The Player, 1992

The Invasion of The Suits, aka *The Body Snatchers*

Every one agrees that The Old Hollywood ceased to exist at some point but people have various opinions as to exactly when that transition happened.

For reasons that will be more fully explained in this chapter, I consider the corporate takeover of The Old Hollywood to be that moment in time when The New Hollywood was born.

As we will detail later in this chapter, The Old Hollywood actually started to fade in the late 1940s but it really disappeared when the New Hollywood became entirely corporate.

Why is that the demarcation line?

The corporate takeover of Hollywood that began in earnest in the 1980s and is complete today has totally changed the entire studio and film making culture.

As with all businesses, the story starts with management and the state of mind of the managers and the people who are dependent on their decisions.

The old time moguls lived, breathed, and dreamed movies. In a way, those moguls were film farmers who delighted in digging their hands in the film soil every day. They championed creative people and made instinctive decisions from their own gut feelings.

That entrepreneurial spirit of filmmaking is the celluloid version of wildcatting for oil, and is anathema to by-the-book corporate thinking.

Entrepreneurs operate from passion, vision, and an almost derisive abandonment of the fear of failure.

Although smaller companies are still often run by visionary risk-takers, most corporate thinking in huge public companies like the ones that own all the studios is more often about finding the safest pathway possible and clinging to it for dear life.

The corporate takeover was the last straw for The Old Hollywood but it was not the sole reason that it disappeared.

So, how did all this happen?

Some of the answers that you will read in this chapter make fairly sweeping statements about the root causes for the emergence of The New Hollywood and the disappearance of The Old Hollywood.

As with all such generalizations, I would be remiss in not noting that there are major individual exceptions and exemptions to many of them.

Goodbye Old Coke, Hello New Coke, Goodbye Coca-Cola

What better company to have started the corporate takeover trend in earnest than Coca-Cola? How delicious is that? (Pun intended.)

It's important to note that Coca-Cola was the company that decided to change the Old Coca-Cola, which people dearly loved, into the New Coca- Cola, which they drank but didn't love, ultimately leading to the re-emergence of the Old Coca-Cola.

Coca-Cola bought Columbia Pictures in 1982 and, just like the New Coke, the deal didn't work out too well so Coke sold Columbia to Sony in 1989.

In 1985, Rupert Murdoch's News Corporation bought Twentieth Century Fox.

In 1986, Ted Turner bought MGM and then almost as quickly sold it back. In actuality, the MGM transition had begun back in 1969 when maverick investor Kirk Kerkorian became the majority shareholder. Through a series of financial maneuvers, MGM ceased being an active movie studio for all intents and purposes during the 1970s, made a brief comeback, and then went dormant again at various times. As such, the roar of the once proud MGM movie lion has been muted for a long time. (In television, MGM was more successful through those years.)

In 1989, Warner Brothers merged with Time,Inc. Time/Warner was then bought by America Online in 2000. What a brilliant synergy that wasn't.

In 1991, Matushita bought Universal which then sold it to Seagram which then sold it to Vivendi which then sold it to General Electric. Whoever repainted the names on studio parking places must have been the busiest person on the Universal lot.

In 1995, Disney took over ABC and overnight became a corporate conglomerate itself.

So, in essence, the huge bulk of the corporate takeover and transition of the major Hollywood studios occurred over a very short period of time, 1982-1995.

And that is the time period during which The Old Hollywood finally morphed itself into Brigadoon and decided to enjoy a temporary leave of absence.

Not for forever.

Not even for a hundred years.

Just for a while.

Like the ill-fated New Coke, The New Hollywood has become something very different from the Old Hollywood.

Corporate. Sterile. Derivative. Devoid of glamour, imagination, and innovation, fueled by marketing tie-ins, endless repetitions of what worked before, and a relentlessly myopic focus on teenagers and adults under thirty.

And mired in a financial model that is now acknowledged even by Hollywood insiders as being irretrievably broken.

I'll Sell You The Studio. No Extra Charge For The Swampland.

As you can see even from some of the transactions we just detailed, the annals of Hollywood are replete with brilliant business people who made fortunes in other businesses, came to conquer Hollywood, and promptly lost their shirts, pants, shoes, underwear, and confidence.

Even a studio like Disney is not immune to that particular malaise.

In 1993, Disney purchased Miramax, the undisputed king of independent films. After Miramax became a corporate entity within a studio structure, it lost its mojo almost overnight and was sold in 2010 (for its library) to private investors.

Multinational corporations like Sony and Matushita have also learned the perils of Hollywood buyouts in a very painful and costly way.

In fact, there was a totally tasteless joke in Hollywood that selling Universal and Columbia at exorbitant prices to those two Japanese companies was American payback for Pearl Harbor.

Ouch.

Murder At MGM

The corporate mentality that now rules every studio has also led to a single-minded reliance on Madison Avenue demographics.

Whereas the giants like Mayer and Thalberg would make films they believed in and order their marketing divisions to come up with ways to sell them, the situation is reversed today.

Marketing executives are consulted on whether the under thirty year-old audience can be lured to theaters by a film. If the marketers are dubious, the film will, in most cases, never see the light of day.

If Indiana Jones were sent to find The Holy Grail in the New Hollywood, his assignment would be to come back with the secret of how a fifteen-year-old boy decides which movies to attend over and over again.

Imagine for a moment Louis B. Mayer in a meeting with his MGM marketing team about *Gone With The Wind* in 1939.

The head of marketing cautions Mayer not to make *Gone With The Wind*. "Sure, it's a big best seller and all, Mr. Mayer, but the teenagers will never go for it and there are no fast food tie-ins."

The next day's headline in *Variety* would have been:

"MGM's Mayer Murders Marketer."

The tail is not wagging the dog.

It has replaced the dog altogether.

A Fever In The Blood

I want to note here that I am not in any way impugning the decency, integrity, or intentions either of the new corporate managers or of business in general.

I believe strongly in the profit motive structure of American business.

In addition, I'm sure that the New Hollywood executives love their families just as much as anyone else and that they would rather have a positive rather than negative impact in the world.

The baseline problem is not intent.

It's orientation.

Asking a left-brained person to make right-brained decisions or vice-versa is a recipe for disaster in any business.

Put more directly, asking a Harvard MBA grad to make creative film decisions is likely to produce the same results as asking a cinematographer to teach nuclear physics.

Hollywood is definitely a business.

That's why the phrase is indeed show business, not show art.

But you have to have the creative pulse of movies circulating in your blood and engrained in your soul or you cannot possibly make the hybrid creative and business decisions that lead to prosperous films.

That does not mean that all movie executives need to be filmmakers. The legendary executives like Thalberg and Mayer were an alchemic blend of businessman, artist, and film devotee.

For these reasons, regardless of good intentions amid daunting challenges, the corporate managers of Hollywood today are pale imitations indeed of the dreams that once fueled the passion of the Laskys, Warners, Thalbergs, Zanucks, and Mayers who pioneered and built the industry.

If any of those moguls came back and saw the way movie decisions are made today, they would feel like a very old and battered pair of brown shoes.

The Loss of Exclusivity

Even though it disappeared only recently, the dimming of The Old Hollywood actually began way back in the late 1940s with the advent of television.

Television ended an almost fifty year uninterrupted run for the film business as the only visual entertainment medium in the world.

Network and local television were followed years later by cable television, super stations, pay-per-view movies, HBO and Showtime, videocassettes, DVDs, video games, computers, the Internet, and more.

In the 1930s, professional sports were only a mere hint of what they are today.

There were sixteen baseball teams in only eleven cities as compared with thirty teams in twenty-seven cities today.

There were eight professional football teams in six cities, compared with thirty-two teams in thirty-one cities today.

Professional hockey has expanded from six teams in the 1930s to thirty teams today.

Professional basketball did not even exist until the mid 1940s and today has thirty teams.

As there was no television, radio was the only medium to which fans could turn to listen to the live, play-by-play action of their favorite teams; that is, sports could only be seen either in person or in highlights on newsreels.

Today, live sports on television are a huge draw twenty-four hours a day.

Not too long ago, people also had to go to the movies to catch up with the latest newsreel so they could actually see news events as they had happened around the world several days or even weeks earlier.

Today, there are several television networks that focus exclusively on news so the never-ending news cycle materializes instantly on televisions and computers twenty-four hours a day.

You Tube videos, which are free and available by the millions, have also become hugely popular and surfing the Internet has become a popular and free of charge form of entertainment in and of itself.

Simply put, where there was little or no competition for visual entertainment as recently as sixty years ago, there are now dozens of viable, exciting, and much less expensive alternatives to a night at the multiplex.

Giving The Inmates Both The Keys and The Deed To The Asylum

For the first fifty or so years of its existence, studios kept one hundred percent of the receipts that they received back from theaters. Much of that money was then funneled back into production.

In 1950, however, James Stewart became the first actor to receive a profit participation in a film (*Winchester 73*).

Even though I can already hear the screaming of the agents (not to be confused with *The Silence of The Lambs*), the advent of sharing profits, and later even grosses, with actors, actresses, writers, directors, and producers marked the beginning of the end of the studio-dominated Old Hollywood structure.

When much of the receipts from a film are siphoned away, there is simply much less money available to put back into production.

To go even further, the advent of profit sharing began the process of focusing more and more on "star power." Salaries escalated into the stratosphere, making movies much more expensive to make, reducing the capital available for production, and ultimately reducing greatly the number of films actually being produced.

In that halcyon year of 1939, studios produced over six hundred films. Today, that number has been reduced by more than two-thirds.

Fewer and fewer films are being made by fewer and fewer stars and directors who are earning much more per film than most actors or directors could even dream of making in their entire lifetime.

As a capitalist, I do not believe that there is anything intrinsically wrong with these New Hollywood astronomical salaries. They just blot out the sun for others who still want to make movies.

And that's another reason for bringing back The Old Hollywood.

Jaws: The Summer Blockbuster is Born Aka The Demise of the Singles Hitters

In 1975, *Jaws* became the first summer blockbuster, the celluloid version of The Emerald City to which every studio thenceforth aspired with almost every decision they made.

That home run mentality brought to an end almost fifty years of studio focus on a balanced slate of films for every audience segment.

Think of baseball becoming a game where the great singles and doubles hitters were all phased out and the only aspiration of every batter in every trip to the plate was to hit a home run. Spurred by that goal, players focus only on strength, no matter what they have to do, or take, to help them hit home runs.

In fact, legalities aside, it could be said that *Jaws* did to film what steroids did to baseball.

Some years ago, a studio head put all this very succinctly to me:

"It's not worth our time anymore to make a film that will only make a solid profit. We need to focus exclusively on films that have the chance to become blockbusters."

Two recent *Wall Street Journal* articles by Ethan Smith about the Disney Company further illustrate the new focus:

"Disney is backing away from one-off comedies…In their place, Disney plans to focus on films that are essentially brands…that can be exploited across its network of theme parks, videogames, and commercial products." ("Disney Narrows its Movie Focus." March 12, 2010.)

"Disney needs to cue some fireworks and show that the overhauled movie division will deliver more blockbusters."("Disney's Movie Division Could Be Wild Card." May 11, 2010.)

Only brand-based features that have the chance to become block-busters.

Successful, profitable films are not enough anymore.

Is Anyone Really Watching?

Astronomically high marketing costs also belie another huge challenge for studios: with the advent of remote controls and TIVO/DVR devices, they don't know who actually sits through television commercials anymore so they have to buy more and more advertising.

Newspapers and print media circulation have fallen off the cliff so those outlets have lost much of their power as advertising outlets for movies.

That leaves the Internet and banner ads on websites but there are no metrics to determine how many Internet users get irritated when they even see banner ads and many web browsers today block pop-up ads.

All in all, it's a new and increasingly expensive undertaking for marketers in The New Hollywood.

And undertaking may be a very appropriate if unsettling choice of words.

Death Knell for Risk Takers:
Sequels, Tie-Ins, and Remakes, Oh My

As we have already mentioned re Disney, more and more studios are today rejecting the whole notion of doing films that don't already have built-in marketing hooks. As a result, sequels and remakes have become the centerpiece of every box office year.

In the spring and summer of 2010 alone, we were subjected to remakes of *The A-Team, A Nightmare on Elm Street, The Wolfman, Clash of The Titans,* and *Robin Hood.* Sequels included *Shrek 4, Iron Man 2, Sex and The City 2, Toy Story 3, Step Up 3, Twilight 3,* and sequels to *Cats And Dogs* and *Nanny McPhee.*

During my old friend and lawyer Tom Pollock's long, successful run as the head of Universal Pictures, one of his early and biggest hits was *Twins,* which featured Arnold Schwarzenegger and Danny DeVito as twin brothers. Later, Tom cast the same two people in *Junior,* which featured Schwarzenegger as the world's first pregnant man. The film bombed.

From an executive's standpoint, Tom made a safe decision because if *Junior* didn't work (and it didn't), he could point to the casting and claim to his bosses that he was not off base in thinking that the same cast that worked in *Twins* would result in another commercial film.

When executives take chances on untried material or personnel, however, and the film fails, those executives have no explanation other than that their personal judgment was wrong.

Of course, their judgment is going to be at wrong at times.

Very wrong. Way wrong. Totally wrong.

Making movies is not rocket science. Regardless of how corporate thinking might want the movie zeitgeist to be, there are no surefire pathways to box office success.

Perhaps the most-repeated and respected one sentence description of the creative process in Hollywood was written by screenwriter William Goldman in his classic book *Adventures in the Screen Trade:* "Nobody knows anything."

The most important support that film executives need to have is the security of knowing that they can fail without getting fired. Without that security, they cannot have the courage to take a shot at a new idea.

With corporate managers and overseers who don't understand, respect, and appreciate the fact that risk taking often fails, executives simply don't have the leeway to crash and burn with new and risky films.

Without that security, we the audience are doomed to an endless film landscape of sequels, remakes, and rehashes of what worked before.

MTV Unleashes The Dark Side of The Force; Technology Outpaces Humanity

A long time ago, in a galaxy far, far away, film editing and directing were all but invisible. The jobs of the director and editor were to design and choose shots that maximized performances by the actors and, more importantly, make the story work.

In 1971, *The French Connection* unveiled a new kind of frenetic editing. Recently, I heard director William Friedkin comment that the film he shot on location for *The French Connection* and the film he actually made of it in the editing room were vastly different.

Ten years later, MTV debuted, ushering in a whole new era that upped the ante on fast-paced editing.

And the dark side of the force was unleashed.

Young directors got the chance to make music videos which by their very nature called for extremely abrupt editing.

The highly coveted youth audience was, of course, the prime demographic of MTV and so studios started hiring those technically adroit young directors to make feature-length films.

At the same time, film schools also jumped into the fray and a whole new generation of film directors was born.

Along with their MTV brethren, these new directors became technical wizards with fast camera moves, dramatic lighting changes, frenzied music, and even more frenetic editing.

Story and performance became secondary as editing quickly became the focus of the videos and films that the new directors made. Technology ruled. In the same vein, many now welcome the emergence of the new 3 D technology, but we can also see this advancement in technology as a further retreat from substance and connection.

Relating to actors and mastering the process of telling a story through performance quickly became a lost art.

A whole generation of directors has thus been created with no experience of actually directing and relating to the human beings through whom stories are told.

In some ways, the current state of technical filmmaking is mirrored in the dependence on technology that many young people have today.

With computers, email, Facebook, Twitter, cell phones, and texting, a whole generation of young people has mastered communicating through technology, but not through the lost art of human communication.

The standard director credit today of "A Film By" is the best evidence of the over-emphasis that The New Hollywood places on directors.

Personally, I believe the so-called possessory credit is an insult to every other person involved in a film. (A director whom I otherwise admire greatly once told me that only directors should be referred to as "film makers." Writers, producers, cinematographers, editors, and others aren't filmmakers? Oh, please.)

"A Film By" credit would never have even been seriously discussed in the Old Hollywood. Films were actually seen for what they are: a collaborative medium through which actors, writers, directors, producers, and crews work together.

Excuse Me: I Don't Want My MTV

So much has been written about The New Hollywood's focus on young audiences that we don't need to spend too much time noting it again.

The key point here is what we noted in Chapter Two: The New Hollywood makes movies about Act One of life and markets them almost exclusively to those who are experiencing Act One in their own lives.

And, you know what, that's great.

Teenagers and kids need a place they can go to be seen and test themselves socially and they should have the opportunity to see films in a group setting that entertain them.

There are, however, hundreds of millions of people around the world who are experiencing Acts Two and Three who just as passionately want to see films that relate to those experiences.

The New Hollywood only rarely addresses those desires today so audiences who are looking for those kinds of films are staying home.

$25 Million: But What About My Dog Trainer?

The soaring salary demands of actors (twenty-five million dollars plus percentage points of the gross for the top stars) and the astronomical cost of television advertising have pushed the *average cost of a Hollywood film to well over one hundred million dollars.*

Yes, that's the *average* cost. It wasn't too long ago that no film even came close to costing that much.

And you read the sentence above correctly. Even though the definition of "gross" varies widely, top stars and directors now get a piece of the *gross* receipts as well.

Those twenty-five million dollar/gross point deals are not even the entire package for the big name stars. Let's not forget the "perks."

The deals for those stars call for several first class round trip tickets to and from the location for the star's family. Assistants, fitness trainers, masseuses/masseurs, drivers, personal make up artists, and hair stylists are also paid for by the studio and premium first class motor homes are also provided.

The crowning "are you kidding me?" lowlight of these deals, however, is the fact that the stars also receive per diems on location that can exceed five thousand dollars per week.

Yes, that is *in addition* to their twenty-five million dollar salaries. Obviously, twenty-five million dollars is not enough money to pay for your own hotel room or food, right?

Of course we're not in Kansas anymore, Toto.

Look, there's a signpost up ahead.

We just entered *The Twilight Zone.*

Who Needs Writers?
"To hell with the script. Let's make a movie!"

The Dramatists Guild for playwrights zealously protects the rights of writers. Even revising the dialogue in a play is no easy task for stage producers or directors.

One of the huge problems with the New Hollywood, however, is that movie story telling (and respect for the written word) has not only become a lost art, it has been all but abandoned.

In The New Hollywood, writers make Rodney Dangerfield look like the most respected man on the planet.

As an illustration, I heard a wonderful story about a plumber who has always wanted to play Hamlet.

For years, he saves money and, finally, using all his savings, he mounts a one-night production at Carnegie Hall in which he plays the melancholy Dane.

Throwing the doors open free to the public, he also invites his family, his friends, and every client for whom he has ever fixed a toilet or a broken water main.

The play begins, and the plumber is simply awful in the role.

After a few minutes, even his friends and family are laughing and some of the public is even booing.

Stopping the production, the plumber speaks to the audience: "Hey, folks. Don't blame me. I didn't write this shit!"

And so it has gone for the art of writing in The New Hollywood.

In The Old Hollywood, studios had extensive story departments and screenwriters were actually respected and much sought after.

Writers, in fact, were revered and the competition to get writers under contract was almost as fierce as the competition for stars.

In the New Hollywood, writers are considered to be highly expendable and somewhat irrelevant. Visual effects, flashy camerawork and editing have supplanted well-written and well-developed dialogue and stories.

Today, it is not unusual to have several writers, most of whom go uncredited, work on one script. Some only write small pieces of screenplays. Some highly paid "script doctors" write only dialogue or just work on one character so that the project will attract a star.

The end result of so many writers on one project is more often than not the same result that would occur if several chefs were hired to cook the same pot of soup.

Spices and other ingredients would conflict with and cancel each other out, leading to an unpalatable blend of cooking styles that would give heartburn to anyone who tasted it.

Where Have You Gone, Story Teller?
The Nation Turns Its Lonely Eyes To You

As a result of the lethal combination of the denigration of writers and the fear of risk taking and other factors in The New Hollywood, technical wizards abound but storytellers are scarce indeed.

The Old Hollywood generation of storyteller directors like Frank Capra, Billy Wilder, Preston Sturgis, Sidney Pollack, William Wyler, Anthony Minghella, and Stanley Kramer are sadly no longer with us.

Wonderful directors like Rob Reiner (*When Harry Met Sally, Stand By Me, The American President*), Francis Ford Coppola (*The Godfather, Apocalypse Now*), Sidney Lumet (*Network, Dog Day Afternoon, The Verdict*), James Brooks (*Terms of Endearment, Spanglish*), Barry Levinson (*Rainman, Good Morning Vietnam, Diner*) and Mike Nichols (*The Graduate, Silkwood, Catch 22*) are still making films but only occasionally.

There are very few directors working today who specialize in character-driven stories with no visual effects.

My old friend Nancy Meyers (*The Holiday, It's Complicated, What Women Want*) and Nora Ephron (*Julie and Julia, Sleepless in Seattle, You've Got Mail*) still proudly carry that torch, as do a very few others like Marc Forster (*Finding Neverland, Stranger Than Fiction*), Cameron Crowe (*Jerry Maguire, Elizabethtown*) and Mike Binder (*The Upside of Anger, Reign Over Me*) but they are in a rapidly dwindling minority. (I personally consider Binder to be the most underappreciated writer/director working in film today.)

Many of us embrace special films that we can watch again and again. The primary reason for our desire to do so lies in the fact that we never tire of spending time with the characters that inhabit that particular film. Characters who are that memorable comfort us and make us feel like we are spending time with old friends. While the actors obviously play a huge role in creating those characters, any actor will tell you that memorable characters are first created by the screenwriter.

Compounding the challenge of making character-driven films is the unfortunate fact that genre directors are given far more latitude and many more chances than directors who make character-driven adult-oriented films.

For instance, Cameron Crowe made the hugely successful *Jerry Maguire* but then stumbled commercially on *Elizabethtown* (which I personally loved) in 2005. Crowe hasn't had a film released since then.

On the other hand, M.Night Shyamalan directed the huge hit *The Sixth Sense* in 1999. After that, he made five other films (*Unbreakable, Signs, The Village, Lady in the Water,* and *The Happening*), all of which fizzled at the box office but studios continued to back his films until he achieved commercial success again with *The Last Airbender* in 2010.

I am not lobbying here against Mr. Shyamalan, whom I admire. I am simply illustrating how treacherous it has become for writer/directors like Cameron Crowe in the New Hollywood.

As the disappointing box office summer of 2010 dragged on, the lack of story emphasis in The New Hollywood was duly noted even by the mainstream media. On June 29, 2010, *USA Today* quoted Brandon Gray of Box Office Mojo: "I think Hollywood didn't even try this summer. They decided to let sequels and spin-offs dominate the summer and didn't worry about story."

"I Sold The Star His New House So I Want a Producing Credit."

In The Old Hollywood, studios and powerful producers such as David O. Selznick were the prime developers of scripts.

Although the New Hollywood still has a few strong and successful soups-to-nuts producers such as Jerry Bruckheimer, Mark Gordon, and Scott Rudin, the producing credit in The New Hollywood has been so denigrated that in March 2010, I noted one film ad that listed six production companies, six co-executive producers, five executive producers, and four producers. Twenty-two producing credits in all.

The prime reason for the decline of the producer has been the massive shift in power away from the studios and producers to actors, directors, and their agents and managers.

For example, there are several personal managers today who get producing or executive producing credits on all the films their clients make, simply because they are managing those stars.

Do I have a prejudice here because of my almost thirty years as a producer?

Of course I do.

But that doesn't change the dynamic at play.

The fate of strong producers in the New Hollywood can best be summed up by the title of David O. Selznick's most famous film: *Gone With The Wind.*

Confusing Darkness with Depth

Anyone who has read film reviews and studied the films that have played in independent theaters over the last several years has seen how dark most independent films have become.

Disclaimer: Anyone should be able to make any film they want if they can get it financed. I am not advocating for these dark films to disappear. Far from it.

My point is that The New Hollywood equates darkness with depth so they make those movies almost to the exclusion of other films. They seem to have lost sight of the fact that there is a desire out here in the audience for films with substance that don't make you feel like you need to take a shower right after the film is over.

The smash 2009 hit *The Blind Side* is a perfect case in point.

Its rousing success was considered a huge surprise in The New Hollywood because it was so hopeful, emotional, and life affirming. Many critics and most of The New Hollywood consider those qualities to be clichés, or too sentimental.

Many of us out here in the audience consider those qualities to be illustrations of who we can be as human beings when we operate at our very best.

Film Critics And The Maytag Repairman

Back in the 1930s, some forever-to-be-anonymous soul sat down with a studio head and suggested that perhaps they should start quoting film critics in newspaper ads for movies.

With that decision, Hollywood started to give power away to film critics, a fateful decision with the unforeseen consequence of certifying a select group of people as the public arbiters of whether a film was worth seeing or not.

Many, if not most, film critics took and still take that responsibility very seriously and do their best to illuminate for their readers and viewers what they consider to be the most important aspects of the film they are reviewing.

Today, however, film critics have much in common with Jesse White, the wonderful old character actor who for many years played a lonely Maytag repairman in television commercials.

Due mostly to the circulation decline of newspapers and the proliferation of the Internet, critics' audiences and influence have both dwindled significantly.

As a result, film critics face some incredibly daunting challenges.

They have to watch every new film that is released by studios and major independents. That means long hours each week in a darkened room watching a lot of movies that are repetitive, amateurish, dark, cynical, violent, exploitative, and just plain awful.

Unlike you and I, they can't just walk out either. They have to stay until the bitter end, both literally and figuratively.

Having to do that week in and week out can quite naturally make some people cynical, jaded, and/or negative. That may at least partially explain why film criticism can often seem quite biting and dismissive.

In addition to the challenges of seeing so many films each week, the steep decline in daily newspaper and weekly magazine circulation has taken a major toll on both the respect for and also the art and sheer numbers of film critics.

Many publications, including the film industry's own *Daily Variety*, have dismissed their film critics altogether. So have countless daily newspapers, national and local magazines, and television stations.

The blazing success of Siskel and Ebert on national television was dimming even before Siskel's untimely death more than ten years ago. Although Ebert had several other partners over the years, the show itself has also now been cancelled.

Another daunting challenge for film critics today is that they have so little influence over a film's fate, particularly in comparison to the days when a handful of New York critics had a huge impact on films.

Back in the 1960s and 1970s, in particular, the critics for *The New York Times, Time Magazine, Newsweek Magazine*, and the three major television networks (CBS, NBC, and ABC), all of whom were New York based, could establish or destroy a film's credibility.

As a result of the other factors we've cited in this section, that influence today is extremely minor; consequently, the critics who are still working at their craft are faced with the reality that the public no longer takes their critiques to heart as they used to do.

Critics can tear apart big commercial films but the public still shows up and even the critics' impact on smaller films has been muted.

As examples, we'll take two films from 2009.

Transformers: Revenge of The Fallen was almost universally panned and even eviscerated by most critics; nevertheless; the film grossed over four hundred million dollars in the United States alone, a figure that was surpassed only by *Avatar*, which became the highest grossing film ever.

Conversely, also in 2009, *The Hurt Locker* was a huge critics' favorite and even won the Oscar for Best Film; however, all the critical accolades it received could not propel it beyond a very lukewarm box office gross.

Critics themselves and The New Hollywood have had to come to grips with the fact both that local and national critics are no longer the force they used to be. For the many critics who still dearly love and appreciate film (such as my sister Susan, Portland Oregonian critic Shawn Levy, and many others), this is a challenging time indeed.

The Internet and The New Hollywood: Fear and Loathing

The Internet has profoundly affected both film criticism and also the actual film production and distribution process in The New Hollywood.

With thousands of websites devoted to film content, people no longer need to wait for the one critic in their area to review a film. Websites such as Rotten Tomatoes give readers a much broader perspective by aggregating dozens of reviews in one place.

Studios also have a very different concern today about film criticism.

Vast expenditures are allotted by studios to open films as successfully as possible. Anything that can impede that opening can threaten the entire chain of a film's commercial trajectory so studios zealously protect films that have not yet opened.

As a result of the proliferation of film websites, however, the democratization of the Internet spreads word so fast that studios have become increasingly paranoid not only about screening films for critics but also even previewing films for test audiences before they are released.

Word of a bad test screening can spread so quickly on the Internet that a film can be labeled a dud months before its release. In Hollywood, as in Washington, D.C., perception can often trump reality.

Harry Knowles, founder of www.Aintitcoolnews.com has become one of the most feared people in The New Hollywood. Knowles gets word of test screenings from informants all over the country and posts them to his hugely successful site. He even sometimes finds out about test screenings beforehand and sends his own "reviewers" to the theater.

Producers and studios used to be able to test films in several different locales with various demographics. Films could thus be honed before they were released. Today, that's a much more dangerous process.

What Dreams May Come was a case in point here. It became clear very quickly that our audience needed closure at a particular point and that our ending was a bridge too far for them. We then reshot the ending, tested the film again, and were relieved to find that the problem was greatly mitigated.

Even though we film makers are often very testy about the weight that studios put on test audience reactions, those screenings can provide invaluable lessons about how a film can benefit from further editing or music changes, etc.

The impact of the Internet on Hollywood has become so profound that *The Hollywood Reporter* and *Variety*, the Hollywood trade publications that were read every morning for decades by almost every one in the industry, have been surpassed in influence by a website. www.DeadlineHollywood.com has now become the "first read" of the industry every morning.

In summary, two radical shifts have occurred because of the Internet:

First, films are often released today with no test screenings, leading to some unpleasant surprises that could easily have been avoided with even one or two audience previews.

Second, audiences, and even many in the industry itself, are paying more attention to user reviews and websites on the Internet than they are to professional critics and traditional Hollywood publications.

The Decline and Fall of The Theatrical Film Experience: Rudeness, Cell Phones, Texting, Ads, and High-Priced Cholesterol

The slide in the fortunes of The New Hollywood can also be traced to the degradation of the theater-going experience itself.

The movie palaces of yesterday have been replaced by mall multiplexes and the new theaters are, in most ways, superior in comfort and viewing to the old theaters.

Audiences, however, are very different today.

Inconsiderate, even rude, behavior is widespread..

People talk to each other during the film as if they were watching television on their couches at home. Even more vexing is that many people actually get very hostile even if they are politely asked to desist.

Cell phones ring and text messages are received and then answered.

In Woody Allen's classic *Annie Hall*, there is a sequence in which Woody is standing in line for a movie, listening to another person pontificate about Marshal McLuhan's media theories. (McLuhan's seminal 1964 book *Understanding Media* coined the phrase "the medium is the message.")

Allen then brings McLuhan himself on camera to tell the pontificator that he is dead wrong about everything he has said about McLuhan's work.

Woody then turns to the camera and says "Wouldn't it be great if real life really went like this?"

In today's theaters, Woody might to have materialize the spirits of Thomas Edison, Alexander Graham Bell, and Emily Post to tell patrons that telephones were not intended to be used in movie theaters so they should "please shut up!"

On screen advertising before movies has also become commonplace today. Until recently, theater owners never had the desperate financial need to screen paid advertising before a film, but that practice is common today.

Besides the annoyance of having to see commercials in theaters, there is also a distinct and potentially damaging subliminal message beneath screen commercials for products like deodorant in movie theaters. They serve to remind people that they can sit home and see commercials so why pay the price to come to a movie theater?

I actually remember the loud booing from audiences when on screen advertising was introduced. On the other hand, younger audiences seem to accept these ads in stride because they do not remember a time when the ads didn't exist.

Ticket prices have also soared and the cost of concessions has become almost comical.

Recently, Lauren and I purchased a small bottle of water at a local chain theater for four dollars and twenty-five cents. That same bottle cost exactly one dollar at a local supermarket two blocks away but then again most theaters have concession police that try to stop you from bringing in your own drinks or food.

It's a dubious distinction but concession prices in theaters have now become as eye-popping as they are in airports. Both are selling products to a captive audience. To be fair to exhibitors, however, their profit margins are so paper-thin that they have to make as much as money as possible on concessions. More on that in a moment.

Many theaters now charge up to six or seven dollars for a box of popcorn with enough industrially manufactured artificial chemicals to clog even the cleanest arteries. Just reading the ingredients could set off alarm sirens at every cardiology office in the neighborhood.

It's not even called butter anymore because it's almost anything but butter. Now it's "butter flavoring", right?

Many years ago, I saw a cartoon in which a man orders a martini at a bar after telling the bartender that it has to be very, very, very dry. The bartender pours the glass full of gin and then simply whispers the word "vermouth" over the glass before handing it to the customer.

The amount of real butter on theater popcorn today has a lot in common with the amount of vermouth in that martini.

And, yes, I hear the cardiologists out there telling me that butter is also bad for us.

But there was nothing like the taste of real buttered popcorn as you watched a movie.

Opera, Rodeos, Corporate Meetings, and The Battle of The Bands: Didn't They Used To Show Movies Here?

It's important to note here that theater owners are absolutely not to blame for the cost issues that we audiences face today when we go to the movies.

In fact, owning an independent theater today must feel a bit like having had all your money invested in pay phones just before cell phones were invented.

For years, theater owners have in fact been just scraping by.

When the cost of property maintenance, personnel, utilities, leases, and such are added to the fact that studio distributors demand incredibly tough deals over box office receipts, most theaters are lucky to just break even on the films they exhibit.

Theater owners basically then have to sink or swim off the concessions they sell. That's why popcorn and other concession prices are so high and why theater managers and ushers are not as vigilant as we might like them to be about unruly patrons. With such meager, if any, profit margins, theaters are very reluctant to discourage anyone from attending a theater.

Many independent theaters have already closed and even the major chain theaters are desperately searching for other events to screen such as The Metropolitan Opera and corporate meetings.

Huge chain multiplexes at least have attractions like 3D. Smaller, independent theaters are facing a daunting combination of high costs and fewer and fewer films that audiences are willing to pay to see in indie theaters.

The studios and all theater owners are facing one similar challenge:

The millions of people who have stopped going to theaters and have instead adopted the mantra of:

"I'll wait until it comes out on Pay-Per-view or DVD."

Those words have become the second most frightening sentence in all of The New Hollywood.

The most frightening?

"Free digital downloads."

Films are now often released on DVD and pay-per-view at home within ninety days of their theatrical release anyway, so the wait is quite short. Theater owners have tried desperately, but unsuccessfully, to lengthen that window so that more people will be motivated to go to theaters, not just wait for the DVD.

In addition, DVD clubs such as Netflix have made it so easy and inexpensive for people to rent and return films that people can sit in the comfort of their own homes and watch films, some on state-of-the-art home theater systems, without the inconsideration of movie audiences.

For a bit over twenty dollars a month, people can rent four movies at a time from Netflix, keep them as long as they want, and change them as often as they want.

One night at one movie, on the other hand, can cost upwards of fifty dollars for a couple, even more if babysitters are involved.

The darker side of even that conundrum is the gigantic black market for pirated films from which studios receive absolutely nothing and to which they lose hundreds of million dollars a year in revenue.

The studios' fear of poor word of mouth on the Internet from a public preview pales in comparison to their terror that someone will sneak a video recording device into a preview screening. Within days, pirated copies of the film could then be available worldwide through the Internet.

"They Said It Was A Comedy: I Guess They Forgot About The Serial Killer."

Another reason that millions of former frequent filmgoers are staying away from theaters is a deluge of blatantly deceptive marketing tactics.

Studios shamelessly scour even terrible reviews of a film so that they can find a few words that will make the review seem positive and also have no compunctions whatsoever about completely misrepresenting the nature of the film itself.

We'll go further into this aspect in Chapter Sixteen.

"We Just Got Out Of The Habit Of Going."

As we discussed in Chapter Three, The Old Hollywood used to be dedicated to a yearlong mix of films for all audience segments.

In The New Hollywood, however, films with substance tend now to be released only in October, November, and December so as to qualify for Academy Awards. While there are a few exceptions, of course, this new pattern means that theatrical fare for the other nine months consists mostly of films for the core under-thirty audience.

As films for other audiences are now basically screened only three months a year, the over thirty audience has simply lost the film-going habit.

They've found something else to do for those nine months: stay home and rent films.

Once that mentality has set in, it then gets increasingly more difficult to get that audience back into theaters at all.

Paging Howard Beale: Triviality Trumps Substance

Remember the times when achieving something artistically actually had to happen before someone was considered a celebrity?

Andy Warhol was more prescient than he could have imagined when he said that everyone in the world would eventually have his or her own fifteen minutes of fame.

Would that it was only fifteen minutes.

Whereas the fan magazines of yesteryear glorified movie and television actors and actresses, the new twenty-four cable stations have created a celebrity culture where truly anyone can lay claim to being a celebrity by simply seeking that celebrity.

No talent whatsoever is required.

Even for legitimate celebrities, the magic and mystique are gone because they are so overexposed so constantly and also because the word "celebrity" has been so denigrated.

Case in point: Kate Gosselin, whose primary "ability" seems to be her willingness to exploit her own children, and whose claim to being a celebrity is rooted only in her desire to be considered as such. Gosselin is, nevertheless, actually referred to as a celebrity by much of the so-called mainstream media.

Gosselin even recently was reportedly paid five hundred thousand dollars to appear on *Dancing With The Stars*.

Meryl Streep is a star. Kate Gosselin? Not so much.

In the classic 1976 film satire *Network*, Howard Beale, a network news anchor, gets so morose over his poor ratings that he threatens to commit suicide on his next broadcast.

Instead, however, the next night he urges all his viewers to go to their windows and scream out to the world:

"I'm mad as hell and I'm not going to take it anymore!"

Of course, his ratings go through the roof.

At that point, the entertainment division of the network takes over the nightly news and turns it into a sideshow that, of course, becomes an ever-bigger success.

Today, the excesses of the celebrity culture have fallen so far into the realm of absurdity that they make the satire of Network look quaint by comparison.

The Holy Grail Changeth:
"TV will save us."
"Cable will save us."
"Videotape will save us."
"DVDs will save us."
"3D movies will save us."
"Is there any new technology left that can save us?"

In the immortal *The Life of Riley* television series of the 1950s, star William Bendix put it even more succinctly:

"What a revolting development this turned out to be."

Put simply and bluntly, the New Hollywood business model is

broken and the question of its survival reverberates daily down every hallway in Hollywood.

Netflix Forecast: DVDS Will Be Gone By 2030

For many years, DVD receipts were the salvation of the New Hollywood bottom line but those receipts have plummeted so precipitously that they no longer can keep The New Hollywood afloat.

The symbolism of Blockbuster Video itself as it teeters on the verge bankruptcy seems to be completely lost on The New Hollywood.

Hollywood Video is already defunct.

Video on demand at home, Red Box video-vending machines, Netflix, and other Internet-based video outlets have done to video stores what DVDs did to videotape.

Netflix's own outlook for the future of DVD industry is startling. In June 2010, Netflix issued a forecast stating that the physical DVD business (sales, rentals via mail, store and kiosk) will disappear completely by 2030.

Can The New Hollywood Survive?

No, it can't, not within its present economic model.

While studios boast of box office receipts, that statistic is bloated because of the steep rise in ticket prices and merely masks the red ink on the bottom line.

Production and marketing costs have ballooned while DVD revenues have plummeted so precipitously that very few films earn back their investments.

While I sincerely hope that they will successfully find their way back through the maze of their current issues, the future of The New Hollywood is not the focus of this book.

My sights are set on bringing back The Old Hollywood, not as a replacement for The New Hollywood, but as its own spirit and entity.

And, with your help, that's exactly what we're going to do.

CHAPTER SIXTEEN

Bringing Back the Old Hollywood

"Life is a state of mind."
Being There, 1979

Fade In.

We're in a family room in the year 2023.

A couple in their mid-fifties are watching one of their favorite films on Turner Classic Movies as their teenage daughter walks in, sits next to them for a moment, and speaks.

"You guys are so cute with your old movies."

"Thanks, honey," Mom laughs.

"Can I ask you something?" the daughter responds.

Putting the film on pause, Dad says "Sure. What's up?"

"It must have been so cool for you guys to have lived during a time when they actually still made new movies every year. What was that like?"

Mom and Dad smile wistfully at each other as Mom responds.

"It was magical. Can you even imagine seeing a brand new film?"

Smiling, the daughter gets up and gives both her parents a hug. "That must have been great. There are only so many old movies you can watch."

"Yeah, we hear that," Dad says.

"Too bad that all ended," their daughter sighs as she walks out.

Mom and Dad look at each and shrug as Dad says:

"Yeah. New movies. Those were the days."

Fade Out.

Endangered Species

Is there really a possibility that new films could actually disappear in the next ten to fifteen years?

Yes, that possibility does exist. Beyond the possibility, is it likely?

The studios of The New Hollywood will hopefully continue to make big event, brand name films, and movies targeted to people under thirty. Assuming their financial model does get fixed (and I hope it does), event films like *Avatar, Transformers, Twilight, Harry Potter,* and any animated movie from the inestimable Pixar, could maintain their places at the multiplex, at least for a while.

Independent films like *Sideways* that primarily appeal to those over thirty are, however, truly an endangered species.

For independent films, the vital signs are indeed flat lining:

Financing sources have dried up.

Theatrical distribution is so difficult that only one out of every two hundred independently financed films ever play in a theater.

Audiences over thirty are staying home.

Due to rising costs, fewer films, and diminished audiences, independent theaters are closing at an alarming rate.

With little or no theatrical presence, the promise of DVD income for a film has all but disappeared.

With no theatrical or DVD presence, there is almost no chance of selling a film to television.

With no U.S. theatrical or DVD distribution, foreign sales are much more difficult if even at all possible.

If something isn't done soon, independent films will certainly become extinct and even the bigger films will be facing an uncertain future.

Only Styrofoam, Cockroaches, And Bad Jokes Last Forever

Lest anyone think that I'm exaggerating the danger, we need look back no farther than several decades to encounter some incredibly popular forms of entertainment that are today either completely defunct or on life support:

Vaudeville.

Silent films.

Burlesque.

Opera.

Ballet.

When they were popular, no one would have thought that any of those art forms could ever be in danger.

That is, until they disappeared or, in the case of opera and ballet, are struggling mightily to stay alive, at least in the United States.

Taking the concept of obsolescence a bit farther:

Would anyone have thought, even as recently as ten or fifteen years ago, that newspapers, magazines, and video stores would be in such dire straits today?

Would you have thought fifteen or twenty years ago that typewriters, non-digital cameras, and pay phones would today be collector's items?

Simply put, a huge segment of filmmaking is indeed in great jeopardy of going the way of eight track tapes.

The survival of new movies is up to us.

The New Plastics: Niches

In the classic 1968 film *The Graduate*, Dustin Hoffman plays a young man who has just graduated from college. Everyone, of course, wants to tell him what to do with his life so, at a party one night, one of the adults takes Hoffman aside and says:

"Benjamin, I'm just going to say one word to you. Plastics."

Certain that he has imparted the secret to future wealth, the man walks away.

If that party occurred today, the word whispered to Benjamin as the key not only to bringing back The Old Hollywood but also to future film business success would have to be "Niches."

Chasing The Elusive Butterfly

Why niches?

The blockbuster mentality that was ushered in by *Jaws* in 1975 has taken a heavy toll on those who have chased the elusive butterfly of its promise as though it were indeed The Holy Grail.

Every once in a while, a movie does come along that captures the fancy of the all age groups and tastes. *Star Wars, Titanic, The Lord of*

The Rings films, the *Harry Potter* films, and *Avatar* are examples of movies that appealed to all audiences.

These films symbolize the pot of gold at the end of the rainbow that has been and continues to be chased by The New Hollywood.

What we don't hear as much about are the hundreds of movies and billions of dollars that have been lost chasing that same elusive butterfly. For example, both *Cutthroat Island* and *The Adventures of Pluto Nash* cost around one hundred million dollars in production alone and neither film grossed even ten million dollars at the box office.

Fueled by their pursuit of mainstream success, studios have made bigger and bigger bets on fewer and fewer films.

The promise of a mainstream blockbuster has caused more filmic shipwrecks than all the seductive sirens ever born.

Of Visionaries and Bass Fishing

Just like their studio corporate cousins, the broadcast networks have also dedicated themselves to a desperate treasure hunt for general audience, mainstream riches.

As a result, networks have also suffered through more than their share of mainstream shipwrecks. Does the television series *My Mother the Car* ring a bell?

As a result of their relentless chase of the elusive mainstream, the so-called big three (ABC, CBS, NBC) networks have lost almost seventy per cent of their audiences since their heyday in the 1960s.

To be fair, some of that loss is due simply to increased competition but much of it can also be attributed to the fact that the broadcast networks keep producing the same sitcoms, crime shows, and medical dramas over and over again.

The sharpest dagger in the heart of mainstream television, however, has been cable television's discovery of the secret of niches.

For instance, most mainstream critics scoffed when both CNN and ESPN were launched as distinct niche networks. The idea of networks devoted only to news or sports was so foreign to the concept of trying to get all eyeballs all the time that very few observers gave either CNN or ESPN much of a chance at survival, let alone success.

CNN was the brainchild of Ted Turner. ESPN was conceived by Scott and Bill Rasmussen. All three entrepreneurs were laughed at and scorned by the so-called mainstream media because they had the temerity to believe that niches were going to be the key to future success in entertainment.

There's a line, spoken by James Mason, in the classic film *Heaven Can Wait* that exquisitely delineates the courage of visionary men and women: "The likelihood of one man being right increases in direct proportion to the efforts of those of who are trying to prove him wrong."

Today, even more distinct new niches are being carved out of the arenas that CNN and ESPN pioneered.

In news, The Fox News Channel and MSNBC have differentiated themselves as conservative and liberal news channels, respectively.

In sports, NBA-TV and the NFL Network are completely devoted to year-round coverage of pro basketball and pro football respectively.

And there's even a bass fishing channel.

Cable is to network television what the niches of The Old Hollywood must become in its new incarnation to the blockbuster mentality of The New Hollywood.

The Spiritual Cinema Circle

In 2004, my business partners Gay and Kathlyn Hendricks, Arielle Ford, Cynthia Litman, and I founded The Spiritual Cinema Circle (www.spiritualcinemacircle.com) as a niche for people who are looking for uplifting and inspiring stories about the human experience.

To The Spiritual Cinema Circle (SCC), the word "spiritual" pertains not to any particular religious belief but to the core nobility and grace of the human spirit. The films that SCC distributes each month look at who we can be as human beings when we operate at our very best; moreover, the most important selection criteria is that each film make us feel better about our humanity.

SCC was a success from the moment we launched in March/April 2004.

In 2006, we sold the majority of the company to Gaiam, Inc. SCC continues to be successful today, with monthly subscribers in almost one hundred countries around the world.

I still participate in choosing the four films that we distribute per month, I host the film discussions on each DVD, and I continue to be the public spokesperson for SCC.

While am very, very proud of the effect that SCC is having in the world, *I note SCC here not as a self-serving advertisement, but rather because it is a practical example of niche entertainment that has become a success in the movie world.*

As niches become more popular in The Old Hollywood, I would expect that subscription movie models such as SCC would also expand in much the same way as subscription models are flourishing in satellite radio, where formats are focused on very specific niches, including, of course, a station totally devoted to the music of Frank Sinatra.

Niches and The Old Hollywood

The film industry already has the rich tradition of horror films as a niche for teenagers looking for thrills at the theater on a Friday night.

I strongly believe that the future of The Old Hollywood will be inextricably linked to creating several niches of films to which audiences and investors over thirty can respond from their own particular interests.

In fact, one of the keys to making the theatrical experience fun again for people will be the opportunity to attend a theater with like-minded, like-hearted, and like-mannered people.

Niches can range from romance to even more specifically targeted romantic comedies to spirituality to politics to relationships to fantasy (without expensive effects) to health to history to family to adult comedy to dance and even to more esoteric niches such as poetry and art.

Many of the niches that will ultimately find the most passionate audiences will be identified by you and the other people who participate in the entertainment summits that we discuss in Chapter Seventeen.

Niches: Seeking Singles and Doubles Hitters

As the New Hollywood focuses only on home runs, The Old Hollywood must seek out films that will be solid singles and doubles.

In baseball terms, this means that home run sluggers like Barry Bonds and Mark McGwire are the heart of the lineup in The New Hollywood while singles and doubles hitters like Tony Gwynn and Richie Ashburn form the core of The Old Hollywood line-up.

Creatively, the home run mentality means that films have to be accessible to almost everyone. Inevitably, this kind of focus leads to a homogenization of the creative process. If all groups are targeted, none can be bored or offended.

On the other hand, creatively making films for niche audiences means that material can be more focused and daring.

To illustrate:

Filmmakers set out to make *The Barack Obama Story* and *The Sarah Palin Story*.

How can make you a mainstream film out of the former without it being a total turnoff to conservatives and how could you produce the latter without it being a total turnoff to liberals?

Answer: you focus on the personal stories of both characters that will resonate with a broad audience, meaning that you absolutely have to stay away from politics in two movies that are about politicians.

You also cast big name stars to play both the leads so you can sell it as an event. (I have no idea who to cast as Obama or Palin but Meryl Streep should play Hillary Clinton. Or maybe she could pull a Peter Sellers in *Dr. Strangelove* and play all the characters.)

End result of a supposedly mainstream movie on Palin and Obama: a very watered down version of both life stories that neither offends nor really pleases anyone. At best, people would leave the theater feeling like hockey fans who spend a lot of money and three hours of their lives watching a game that winds up in a tie.

If, however, you know you have a liberal niche audience for Obama and a conservative niche audience for Palin, you make each movie on a modest budget with no big name actors and only the core audience in mind. You can then jump headfirst into the political stories, knowing that you will be pleasing the specific audience for whom you are making the film.

You would just have to be certain that you don't mistakenly send the Palin film to San Francisco or the Obama film to Salt Lake City.

Translated to film terms, what this new focus would mean is a return to solid and sane business practices.

While The New Hollywood spends hundreds of million dollars looking for the big score, The Old Hollywood needs to be focused on modestly budgeted films with proven niche audiences.

Making a solid if unspectacular profit on a slate of niche films will be a huge boon to all concerned.

Investors will be encouraged that they're on solid footing once again; filmmakers, actors, and crews will be working more; and audiences will enjoy niche films that are specifically tailored for them.

For Investors: Niches Rhymes With Riches

(Unless you're in France where the pronunciation would be "neeshes' which would only rhyme with "quiches" and that is a whole other business altogether.)

Anyway, the point to be made here is that the niches will attract filmmakers and investors who feel aligned personally with a particular niche and want to support it with their talents and investments.

The Old Hollywood Will Not Replace The New Hollywood: Frozen Fish and Hot Waffles

It's crucial to note that the Old Hollywood has to be its own separate entity. It cannot and should not try to replace or compete with The New Hollywood.

Carl Sandburg had a wonderful phrase that illustrates the importance of that very crucial distinction:

"Telling a frozen fish that it is a hot waffle does as much good as telling a hot waffle that it is a frozen fish."

The New Hollywood (frozen fish) focuses on big stars, big salaries, big budgets, and general audience films that appeal primarily to people under thirty.

The Old Hollywood (hot waffle) should focus on a return to story telling, financial sanity, actors and actresses that are chosen for their talents (not the likelihood that their names will guarantee DVD presales in Germany), and subject matter that appeals primarily to people over the age of thirty.

The New Hollywood is firmly rooted geographically in Southern California and economically in the paradigm of the multinational corporations who own and operate the studios and major independents.

As there will be little if any synergy between the New and Old Hollywood, there is absolutely no reason that The Old Hollywood should have to be located only in Southern California.

There are thousands of talented people who desperately want to make films but, for whatever personal or lifestyle reasons, want to live and work elsewhere. As doing so is a very difficult challenge for all but the top tier actors and directors in The New Hollywood, The Old Hollywood should embrace geographical diversity with open arms.

Today, there are vibrant film communities in Florida, Texas, New

Mexico, Oregon, Washington, Illinois, New York, Louisiana, and Connecticut, just to name a few in the United States.

In Canada, Vancouver and Toronto have incredibly active film communities and, around the world, there are more film communities than can possibly be enumerated here.

India, for instance, produces over one thousand films every year.

There is no reason, of course, that the renaissance of The Old Hollywood cannot also take root in Southern California but it would be just one root of an ever-expanding tree.

Probably not a palm tree.

In Bollywood We Trust

As the niches of The Old Hollywood become better defined, it's also entirely possible that certain geographical regions will become more intimately linked with a certain niche or two, thereby attracting both the talent and investors who share an interest in that niche.

Using India as an example, Bollywood is often considered to be synonymous with the entire Indian film industry. It is, however, but one of the many different styles of Indian films and is centered in Mumbai, while other areas around India produce other niche films.

What does not yet exist is a mechanism through which all of those communities and niches can be interlinked, not by the restrictions of The New Hollywood, but by the desire of filmmakers and investors all over the world to connect with each other and audiences through niche films that do not fit into The New Hollywood paradigm.

Rebirthing Respect for and Trust From Audiences

"No one ever went broke underestimating the intelligence of the American public." H.L. Mencken.

"There's a sucker born every minute." P.T. Barnum.

Many former filmgoers now completely and justifiably mistrust the Hollywood marketing machine that has become so myopically focused on opening weekend grosses that it will say and do almost anything to put people in the seats.

Mass marketing of theatrical films on television is a relatively recent phenomenon that began in the 1970s. Before that, films opened with publicity campaigns but very little if any paid advertising. The explosion of the popularity of network television in the 1970s, however, ushered in the new era of massive advertising campaigns and budgets that put increasing pressure on marketers to guarantee huge opening weekend box office grosses.

That pressure not only caused marketing costs to skyrocket, it also led to some very deceptive ad campaigns that lured people into movies under false pretenses.

When that happens, people feel exploited by the process, making them much less interested in coming back again.

As we noted in Chapter Fifteen, studio marketers have absolutely no problem taking a few words from a highly negative review of a film and making them seem like a rave endorsement. For this reason and others, audiences cast a very suspicious eye on review quotes.

Deceptive advertising and promotion is by no means restricted to taking reviews out of context. Studios often completely misrepresent the nature of the film itself.

Example one: *The Blair Witch Project.*

Filmgoers (and critics) were led to believe that the film included real footage of actual events when, in truth, it was completely fictional. As a supposedly real experience, audiences were fascinated by the film; however, when it became known that the film was a hoax, many people felt exploited and still others saw the film as far less entertaining.

Example two: *Pay It Forward.*

On the heels of his huge success in *The Sixth Sense*, Haley Joel Osment became quite a popular young star, much in the mold of Macauley Culkin from *Home Alone.*

Pay It Forward, Osment's first feature after *The Sixth Sense*, was sold as a feel-good film for all audiences, neglecting the small, insignificant detail that Osment's character is actually beaten to death at the end of the film. I personally knew several parents who had to take shocked and sobbing youngsters out of the theaters.

The Old Hollywood needs to remember that The New Hollywood has lost the faith of many people who no longer trust that a film will be what it is advertised to be.

"Fool me once, shame on you."

"Fool me twice, shame on me."

"Fool me several times a year, and I'm staying home from now on."

"Show Me The Money!"

Speaking of trust, films have acquired such a toxic reputation as an investment that a whole new paradigm of trust between investors and filmmakers needs to be constructed.

On one side of the coin, filmmakers are so sick of studio accounting skullduggery that they don't trust the process at all. Legendary studio accounting maneuvers have made net profits as plentiful as white crows.

On the other side of that same coin, finding investors for independent films has become so difficult that filmmakers are mostly restricted to their families, friends, and their own credit cards for financing.

Accordingly, there is much work to be done so that investing in independent films can become attractive and available again.

A New Alliance of Filmmakers, Financiers, and Theaters

One of the exciting challenges of bringing back The Old Hollywood will be to create that mechanism through which individual communities can share information, innovation, and resources without losing their unique identities.

Right now, the domestic film world has to go to The New Hollywood for theatrical distribution, the process through which the studios have been able to maintain their stranglehold on American film distribution. To date, subsequent distribution streams such as DVD and cable have been defined by theatrical distribution, which in turn has been completely controlled by the major studios.

With a new alliance of filmmakers, financiers, and theaters working outside that paradigm, new financing and distribution channels can be forged that do not funnel through the studios.

Getting Back Into the Habit

In The New Hollywood, that would mean casting Julie Andrews in a sequel to *The Sound of Music.*

In The Old Hollywood, it means bringing people back into movie theaters.

As we detailed in Chapter Fifteen, the theatrical experience has become very challenging for theater owners and for large segments of the audience.

As someone who has spent thousands of hours in movie theaters,

I hope and believe that we can find a way to preserve that experience. To accomplish that goal, filmmakers, audiences, and theaters that want to save the theater-going experience desperately need each other now.

The Majestic Power of Story

Together, writers, directors, and producers need to rediscover the majestic power of story telling that has been an essential aspect of the human heart and experience since our cave dweller days. At the dawn of humanity, people gathered around fires to listen enraptured to the stories of tribal leaders and shamans.

Those leaders and shamans passed on the myths (epic stories, not fabrications) of their culture through the magic of story telling.

Stories enrich our lives, fire our imaginations, and engage our hearts in a very special and uniquely human alchemy.

Filmmakers today are among the twenty-first century versions of those campfire storytellers from our distant past.

The light of the fire is now projected on a movie or television screen and is reflected in the yearning of our hearts to be reignited with hope.

While The New Hollywood uses technology to illuminate epic stories, The Old Hollywood should illuminate our humanity through traditional story telling that holds us in its thrall and makes our spirits soar.

For the last several years, HBO (*The Sopranos, John Adams*, etc.) has become the pre-eminent producer and distributor of quality, character-oriented, and story-based filmmaking. In fact, cable television has for the time being surpassed theatrical films as the most consistent delivery system for films about Acts Two and Three of life.

As a natural extension of the rebirth of story telling, character development, and a preference for our humanity, screenwriters should again be respected as the talented artists they are, directors need to rediscover the lost art of communicating with actors, and a whole new and mutually respectful synergy needs to be created among writers, producers, and directors.

An Emphasis on Our Humanity, Not Our Technology

As with society itself, the magic of story telling (humanity) has been overrun by advances in film technology.

Many of us feel that the modern onslaught of technology has been so pervasive that our hearts and souls desperately need a breather.

Do we want our humanity to be controlled by our technology or the other way around?

Just because we can do something technologically does it mean that we *should?*

In 1968, the brilliant Stanley Kubrick gave us a preview of the dangers of human reliance on technology in *2001: A Space Odyssey.* In the film, a spaceship is run by a computer called Hal 9000. When questioned about its reliability, the computer responds:

"The 9000 series is the most reliable computer ever made. No 9000 computer has ever made a mistake or distorted information. We are all, by any practical definition of the words, foolproof and incapable of error."

Right after that, the computer terminates the life support systems of the crew who are in suspended animation, kills another while on a mission outside the ship, and then attempts to murder the last remaining crewman before he can disconnect the computer's brain.

By eschewing a reliance on technology and big budgets, The Old Hollywood will have the freedom to explore films that give our humanity a chance to at least catch up with our technology.

And, who knows, maybe the depth of our humanity can even once again surpass the limits of our technology.

What dreams may come, indeed.

Movies On The Internet: Here To Stay or Fleeting Trend?

One of today's raging debates revolves around the possibility of the Internet becoming the prime delivery mechanism for movies.

People under thirty are so accustomed to watching entertainment, including movies and television, on their computers that an assumption is growing that the Internet will soon become the single biggest and most important distribution outlet for movies.

There is no question that most of us over the age of forty were not raised in the computer age; therefore, we don't have a history of downloading movies and watching them on our computers. An important question for us baby boomers and generation x-ers then is whether or not we will adopt the habit of downloading films to watch them on our computers.

A further assumption being made is that boomers and x-ers will eventually pass from the scene, thereby eliminating all resistance to the

Internet becoming the prime distributor of films.

I believe that the far more intriguing question revolves around the pervasive power and influence of the Internet itself. Whether or not the Internet overall will continue to dominate the way it has over the last ten or fifteen years is certainly an intriguing debate to have.

For those of who love movies, however, the questions become much more specific:

Will boomers and x-ers "get with the movie program" on the Internet?

Will young people who watch movies on their computers continue to do so as they age, as many are now assuming? Or will the isolation of the technology affect them later in life as well?

Simply put, what if the experience of watching movies on computers is only a passing trend?

Many people seem to automatically assume that the Internet will now dominate movie entertainment until the end of time.

Maybe it will, but what if it doesn't?

Remember silent movies, vinyl albums, eight track tapes, VHS, AM and CB radio, and Blockbuster?

I expect this to be one of the more lively debates at the coming entertainment summits (Chapter Seventeen).

A Species That Consciously Loves and Forgives

"Beware the beast Man, for he is the Devil's pawn. Alone among God's primates, he kills for sport or lust or greed. Yea, he will murder his brother to possess his brother's land. Let him not breed in great numbers, for he will make a desert of his home and yours. Shun him; drive him back into his jungle lair, for he is the harbinger of death."
Planet Of The Apes, 1968

"Shall I tell you what I find beautiful about you? You are at your very best when things are worst."
Starman, 1984

If we survey the predominant ethos of the last couple of decades of film, we might have to conclude that *Planet of The Apes* had it right.

If, however, we examine the films of The Old Hollywood, and what they can be again, we know that the *Starman* perspective can prevail.

By ignoring the technological obsession of The New Hollywood, The Old Hollywood can give us a moment to rediscover our humanity.

In so doing, we just might remember some of our beauty as a species, rather than just our darkness.

While I do not ascribe to the ostrich theory of not looking at our darkness, I also believe that some balance is desperately needed.

Yes, we can be greedy, cruel, and violent.

We also, however, can be kind, compassionate, loving, and forgiving.

I am not suggesting that the Old Hollywood should be a Pollyanna balance to The New Hollywood. Not at all.

The new films of The Old Hollywood should, will, and must continue to investigate and illuminate the heart of darkness; however, there should be a balance for people who are looking for hope and inspiration.

Forever Thirty-Nine: *Soylent Green*

Jack Benny wasn't the only person who couldn't bear the thought of turning forty.

I have an old, uh, long-time friend who worked very successfully for many years as a writer in The New Hollywood.

One of the most extraordinary aspects of my friend's success was that he somehow managed to stop the aging process. When he reached thirty-nine, he just magically stayed there for almost a decade.

As the executive revolving door continued to spin, and new faces appeared, he just stayed thirty-nine. Unlike *The Picture of Dorian Gray*, he didn't have a rapidly aging portrait stashed in an attic somewhere.

When you hit forty in The New Hollywood, you are looked upon much like a milk carton that has exceeded its expiration date.

If you have the temerity and incredibly bad judgment to actually turn fifty and admit it, many people look at you as though you were auditioning for the next sequel to *The Night of The Living Dead*.

In short, despite a successful class action lawsuit a few years ago, ageism is almost a religion in The New Hollywood.

Sadly enough, people's careers often hinge on looking and behaving younger and younger as they get older and older; hence, the plethora of plastic surgeons in Los Angeles.

Whereas age and experience are qualities that are respected and even revered in many cultures and societies, those same qualities are the kisses of career death in The New Hollywood; therefore, they must be camouflaged and hidden from sight.

Soylent Green was a 1973 science fiction film that posited a future where food had become so scarce that human beings were recycled into a new food called Soylent Green. A remake of that film is now in development. So, to writers, actors, directors, and producers over forty: caution--we may be next. *Soylent Gray*, anyone?

Practically speaking, though, it's completely understandable that a business that caters almost exclusively to teenagers and people in their twenties would prefer writers, directors, actors, and producers who relate to the issues of that audience.

It's beyond pathetic, however, for talented people over forty to have to pretend that they are something that they are not and it's even worse for those people to have to come up with movie ideas that don't in any way appeal to them or their life experiences anymore.

As The Old Hollywood focuses on Acts Two and Three of life, it will be the beneficiary of the talents of thousands of men and women whose creative passions have been stifled by the New Hollywood. When those passions are released and then channeled into films that are no longer limited to teenage angst, the force of the creative outpouring from these talented filmmakers will make a hurricane feel like a mild breeze.

The Light Is Better Here

Someone walks into a house to find that it is pitch dark except for one light in the corner of the living room. They see a friend crawling on hands and knees under that one light.

"What's going on?"

"I'm looking for my keys."

"Are you sure you dropped them right there?"

"No, I'm pretty sure I dropped them on the other side of the room but the light is better here."

I tell that story here because I'm fully aware that the discussions I've started in this book about bringing back The Old Hollywood are mostly illuminated by the light of what I can see in that one corner of the room.

The most important keys may very well lie hidden in one of the other three corners that for me remain in the shadows.

Perhaps you know where that light switch is located so that together we can find a way to illuminate the entire room.

There's a Chinese proverb that says, "May you live in interesting times." I have always understood that to mean that living in times of turbulence and change is an opportunity that lets us appreciate the great gifts that life reveals to us when we're willing to look in the corners that are not as well lit.

And these certainly are interesting times.

"I know how hard it is in these times to have faith. But maybe if you could have the faith to start with, maybe the times would change. You could change them. Think about it. Try. However hopeless, helpless, mixed up and scary it all gets, it can work."

Oh, God, 1977

If we believe in ourselves and our humanity, together we can now forever change the destiny of movies.

I invite you to join me in that quest.

CHAPTER SEVENTEEN

PLEASE JOIN OUR COMMUNITY
AT
WWW.THEOLDHOLLYWOOD.COM

"If you build it, they will come."
Field of Dreams, 1989

Together, We Can Bring Back The Old Hollywood.

Meet Us At The Summit

Bringing Back The Old Hollywood is not just a metaphor.

It is, rather, a practical and achievable goal.

To do so is going to require the establishment of a new marketplace where people who care about the future of movies can gather to discuss, debate, and decide how movies outside The New Hollywood will get financed and distributed from this moment forward.

When local issues are in need of airing, town halls are often convened so that every one in the community can have a voice in the outcome.

When major world issues are at stake, a summit is often convened to determine how to proceed.

Combining the best of both those worlds, we are now planning film summits with a town hall atmosphere and structure.

These new film summits will not convene in just one physical location because The Old Hollywood cannot return in just one place.

The new town hall summits on the future of filmed entertainment will meet online and in various cities around the world where film communities are already burgeoning and where more will proliferate as the next few years unfold.

These town hall summits are already in the planning phase for several cities and await your participation and input as to how they will look, feel, and be.

The purpose of this brief final chapter is to call those town summits and participants to action.

Chapters Fifteen and Sixteen delineated some of the issues that I believe will need to be discussed at the summits; however, *many of the solutions to the challenges weren't addressed in those chapters because I'm simply not smart enough to have thought of all of them.*

Those solutions will have to come from you.

For all these reasons and more, we invite and look forward to your input and participation in the process.

A New Coalition

The summits will bring together a new and vibrant coalition of writers, producers, financiers, directors, actors, actresses, executives, crew members, distributors, media, film lovers, lawyers, theater owners, and supporters from all over the world.

The integrity of the structure of the summits depends on avoiding a lecture format of any kind. In other words, there will be no top down pontificating from someone claiming a superior position or knowledge.

This process is in many ways a huge jigsaw puzzle that awaits the delivery of individual pieces from people around the world.

For those reasons, the summits will be scheduled and physically designed in venues where every one who comes to participate will indeed have the opportunity to do so.

Adams, Jefferson, Hamilton, and Madison

My vision for these summits actually took shape watching the brilliant HBO miniseries *John Adams*.

Delegates appeared from every colony to sit down together and form a new republic. The process was often messy, the discussions were passionate, and opinions varied greatly on how to proceed until consensus eventually emerged and a course of action was determined.

In other words, participants waded into the maelstrom of creativity and didn't emerge until a new vision eventually appeared.

The Journey Begins

Expanding on the overview of The Old Hollywood in Chapter Sixteen, we can use the outline below as a starting point. If you have a particular interest in any of these areas, please consider joining one of the committees that are working on various aspects of our mission:

NICHES

The New Plastics: The Key to The Kingdom
Mainstream: The Elusive Butterfly
The Spiritual Cinema Circle
Niches and The Old Hollywood
Niche Writers, Directors, and Producers
For Investors: Niches Rhymes With Riches

CREATIVITY

The Old Hollywood Will Not Replace The New Hollywood
Screenwriter and Story Telling Renaissance
The Rebirth of Character-Driven Films.
An Emphasis On Our Humanity, Not Our Technology.
A Species That Consciously Loves and Forgives.
Directors Who Respect and Know How to Communicate With Actors
How Many DVDs Can We Sell In Germany With That Cast?
Producers Who Produce
Forever Thirty-Nine: *Soylent Green*

STRUCTURE

Separate And Equal Regional Filmmaking Centers
A New Alliance of Filmmakers, Financiers, and Creative Forces:
Companies That Focus on Filmmaking, Not Theme Parks,
Product Placement, Merchandising Tie-ins, or Cross-Platforming

FINANCING: SHOW ME THE MONEY!

Re-establishing Trust Between Investors and Filmmakers
Profit Participation
Nonprofit Encounters Of the Intentional Kind
Investor/Filmmaker Incentives
A Return to Modest Budgets
Help Wanted: Seeking Singles and Doubles Hitters
A New Financial Partnership With Theaters

DISTRIBUTION AND MARKETING

Rebirthing Respect for and Trust From Audiences
An End To The Tyranny of Opening Weekend
Getting Back Into The Habit Again
Wined, Dined, And Wooed: Making Theaters Fun
Movies on The Internet: Here to Stay or Passing Trend?

An Invitation

So, no matter whether you are a filmmaker or a movie fan, we invite you to join us at www.TheOldhollywood.com

Welcome home, Old Hollywood.
We missed you.

Acknowledgements, Excuses, and Mea Culpas

First, to my wonderful kids and granddaughter, I send my love and eternal gratitude for being who you are and also for allowing me to share your journey through this incredible adventure we call life. Family, you are the best. Oh, and one of you (except Carter who's only fourteen) better start working on that next grandchild or Lauren will be advertising for potential fathers on your Facebook pages.

Next, I want to acknowledge my memory. Thanks for the help and you better be right or, like Lucy Ricardo, we'll have a lot of explaining to do.

In all transparency, some of my recollections could be spotty, like maybe an event happened in a different year. Some of the conversations that I quote are my own dramatic reconstructions of those moments, rather than a claim of verbatim, court reporter accuracy.

As to any other errors or gaffes, the responsibility lies squarely on the shoulders of Stephen Deutsch who left me a lot of messes to clean up when he disappeared in 1996. Last time I heard, he had entered the witness protection program and was working as a booking agent for circus performers in Uzbekistan.

As much as possible, I have tried to verify incidents with those who were there with me. Huge hugs go to my sister Susan Granger, Nancy Meyers, Don Granger, Michael Dellar, Dr. Stephen Renzin, Jeannot Szwarc, Andrew Fogelson, Pete Carroll, Michael Chapman, Pat McCorkle, Mort Engelberg, James Mapes, Dan Dewey, Ann Rutherford Dozier, Steve Ellis, Jo Addie, Bill Shepard, and many others for your kindness and patience.

To those I tried to reach but who didn't respond: Hey, I tried! In addition, I did not discuss every film with which I was involved in my career simply because I did not think that those experiences fit into either the narrative or timeline of the book. A more complete credit list (the good, the bad, and the ugly) is included in the "About The Author" section.

Special thanks to my mentor Richard Matheson who inspired me to become the man I had always wanted to be. I'm still working on it, Richard.

Huge gratitude to my friend and business partner Gay Hendricks whose wisdom, friendship, and guidance have changed my life forever.

Love and eternal thanks to my soul brother Neale Donald Walsch, who got me out of Los Angeles and literally revived both me and my family when we needed it most.

I would have been completely lost without the Internet Movie Database. www.imdb.com. For those of you have any questions about a film, its star, or whatever, www.imdb.com is absolutely the place to go.

Thanks also to Wikipedia, the online encyclopedia, for invaluable information about people, places, events, and timelines.

Special thanks to my friend and brilliant lawyer Cynthia Litman and her equally brilliant husband Craig. Your advice and friendship is a constant source of comfort and encouragement. Oh, and my apologies to Cynthia for being such a pain in the you-know-what.

A huge nod to Andrew Green of Green Solutions for coordinating the publishing and printing of the book, fulfilling orders for it, and also for his generous heart. And to Shirley Green for a Herculean job of proof reading.

A big round of applause to Greg Traver for his incredible design of the book covers (front and back) and interior layout.

Much gratitude to Pausha and Chris Foley for their wonderful design for and construction of www.TheOldHollywood.com.

Huge hugs to our beloved Labrador Lola and our eccentric cats Salem and Sophie for always reminding me about unconditional love and affection.

There are no words that can adequately express my adoration for my beautiful, amazing wife Lauren whose unconditional love is the most cherished gift of my life.

And my deepest gratitude to those Old Hollywood ghosts and spirits who visited me often while I was writing this book and inspired me to call them home once again.

About the Author

Stephen Simon was born into a successful Hollywood family. His father, S. Sylvan Simon, was a producer/director who made films with stars such as Abbott and Costello, Lana Turner, and Red Skelton. He worked as both a producer and an executive at Columbia Pictures under the legendary Harry Cohn, producing films such as *Born Yesterday*, the 1950 film that garnered a Best Actress Oscar for star Judy Holliday.

Sylvan Simon died when Stephen was four years old, an event which compelled Frank Sinatra to become Stephen's "godfather".

Stephen's mother Harriet remarried Armand Deutsch, a film producer at MGM who produced films with stars such as Robert Taylor, James Stewart, and Grace Kelly. Armand Deutsch adopted Stephen, changing the young boy's last name to Deutsch.

In 1996, Stephen legally changed his name back to Simon.

In more than thirty years as a producer, director, and production executive, Stephen has been involved in the production of over twenty films.

Stephen personally produced such acclaimed projects as the Academy Award® winning *What Dreams May Come* (starring Robin Williams and Cuba Gooding Jr.), the cult classic *Somewhere in Time* (Christopher Reeve and Jane Seymour), and *All The Right Moves* (Tom Cruise).

Stephen was also co-executive producer on fan favorites *Bill and Ted's Excellent Adventure* and *Bill and Ted's Bogus Journey* (Keanu Reeves), produced *She's Out of Control* (Tony Danza), executive produced *Body of Evidence* (Madonna), produced the first original film to premiere on the Internet (*Quantum Project*), starring John Cleese and Stephen Dorff, was an executive producer on *Linda McCartney* for CBS Television, and was nominated for an Emmy Award as one of the executive producers of *Homeless to Harvard* for Lifetime Television.

Stephen was the head of production of the film companies owned by legendary Hollywood producers Ray Stark (*Funny Girl, The Goodbye Girl, The Way We Were*) and Dino De Laurentiis (*Serpico, La Strada, 3 Days of The Condor*).

As an executive, Stephen supervised the development and/or production of films such as *Smokey and The Bandit, Army of Darkness, Kuffs, The Cheap Detective, Russkies, The Gate, Murder by Death, The Wraith, Casey's Shadow, Once Upon a Crime,* and *The Electric Horseman.*

Stephen directed and produced *Indigo* and the film version of *Conversations with God.*

In 2004, Stephen co-founded The Spiritual Cinema Circle (www.spiritualcinemacircle.com), a monthly DVD distribution service that became an immediate international success, with subscribers in 2010 in almost one hundred countries.

Stephen has been a voting member of the Academy of Motion Pictures Arts and Sciences since 1984.

Stephen's first book, *The Force is With You,* was published by Hampton Roads in 2002.

Stephen has led seminars and workshops throughout the United States and Canada and has appeared on dozens of radio and television programs.

Stephen earned his Bachelor of Arts Degree from UCLA in 1971 and a Law Degree from Loyola Law School in Los Angeles in 1974. After being admitted to the California Bar in 1974, he practiced law briefly in Los Angeles before entering the film industry in 1976.

Stephen's sister is well-known film critic Susan Granger.

Stephen resides near Portland, Oregon with his wife Lauren, two of their six children, two cats, and a dog.

INDEX